BEST EDITORIAL CARTOONS

OF THE YEAR

2014 EDITION

STEVE BREEN
San Diego Union-Tribune

BEST EDITORIAL CARTOONS OF THE YEAR

2014 EDITION

Edited by
DEAN P. TURNBLOOM

Text by
CHARLES G. BROOKS, JR.

PELICAN PUBLISHING COMPANY
GRETNA 2014

Dedicated to the memory of Charles Brooks, Sr.,
who edited this series for forty years

Library of Congress Serial Catalog Data

Best Editorial Cartoons, 1972-
Gretna [La.] Pelican Pub. Co.
v. 42 cm annual—
"A pictorial history of the year."

United States—Politics and Government—
1969—Caricatures and Cartoons—Periodicals.
E839.5.B45 320.9'7309240207 73-643645
ISSN 0091-2220   MARC-S

Printed in the United States of America

Published by Pelican Publishing Company, Inc.
1000 Burmaster Street, Gretna, Louisiana 70053

Contents

Award-Winning Cartoons

2013 PULITZER PRIZE

STEVE SACK

Editorial Cartoonist
Star Tribune, Minneapolis

Attended the University of Minnesota; cartoonist for the *Star Tribune* since 1981; recipient of numerous awards for cartooning, including the Sigma Delta Chi Award, 2003, the National Headliner Award, also in 2003, the Scripps Howard Journalism Award, 2004, and the Berryman Award, 2006; according to the cartoonist, "My job description is simple. I read the paper, crack a joke, and draw a picture."

2013 NATIONAL HEADLINER AWARD

STEVE BREEN

Editorial Cartoonist
Union-Tribune, San Diego

Born in Los Angeles in 1970; graduate of the University of California at Riverside, 1992; editorial cartoonist for the *Asbury Park Press* (N.J.), 1996-2001, and the *Union-Tribune,* 2001 to the present; winner of the Pulitzer Prize, 1998 and 2009, the Berryman Award, 2007, the Thomas Nast Award, 2009, and the National Headliner Award, also in 2009; his comic strip "Grand Avenue" appears in more than 150 newspapers; author of several children's books.

2013 JOHN FISCHETTI COMPETITION

MATT BORS

Editorial Cartoonist
Medium

Graduate of the Art Institute of Pittsburgh, 2003; nationally syndicated political cartoonist at *Medium,* where he edits a comics collection, "The Nibs"; also winner of the 2012 Herblock Prize for Cartooning and the 2011 Sigma Delta Chi Award.

2013 THOMAS NAST AWARD

ROB ROGERS

Editorial Cartoonist
Pittsburgh Post-Gazette

Editorial cartoonist in Pittsburgh for three decades; curator of several national cartoon exhibitions; winner of the National Headliner Award, 1995, and previous winner of the Thomas Nast Award for editorial cartoons, 2000; author of *No Cartoon Left Behind: The Best of Rob Rogers;* serves as board president of ToonSeum, a cartoon museum in Pittsburgh.

2013 HERBLOCK PRIZE

DAN PERKINS

aka TOM TOMORROW

Editorial Cartoonist
This Modern World

Draws under the pen name Tom Tomorrow; creator of the weekly comic strip "This Modern World," which appears on Daily Kos, at TheNation.com, and in some 80 newspapers nationwide; editor of the comics section he created for Daily Kos; recipient of the Robert F. Kennedy Journalism Award for Cartooning, in 1998 and 2003.

2012 SIGMA DELTA CHI AWARD
(Newspaper circulation below 100,000)
(Selected in 2013)

PHIL HANDS

Editorial Cartoonist
Wisconsin State Journal

Born in Syracuse, New York, 1980; graduated from Kenyon College with degrees in political science and art, 2005; earned master's degree in journalism from the University of Wisconsin, 2008; served as cartoonist for the *Pittsburgh Press* and the *Pittsburgh Press-Gazette;* joined the staff of the *Wisconsin State Journal* in August 2013; while his cartoons frequently tackle national issues, they generally are crafted specifically for a Wisconsin audience; often described as a fierce political moderate, he is inclined to attack extremists wherever he finds them.

2012 SIGMA DELTA CHI AWARD
(Newspaper circulation above 100,000)
(Selected in 2013)

SCOTT STANTIS

Editorial Cartoonist
Chicago Tribune

Born in San Diego, California; editorial cartoonist for the *Chicago Tribune* since 2009; previously was staff cartoonist at the *Grand Rapids Press;* the *Arizona Republic,* the *Orange County Register,* and the *Birmingham News;* cartoons are syndicated in more than 400 newspapers; creator of the internationally syndicated comic strip "Prickly City"; past president of the Association of American Editorial Cartoonists.

BEST EDITORIAL CARTOONS OF THE YEAR

2014 EDITION

JOKE

Apologies to Shepard Fairey

caglecartoons.com

TAYLOR JONES
Caglecartoons.com

The Obama Administration

The troubled rollout of Obamacare was just one of the ongoing problems that beset the White House in 2013. Questions about the Benghazi attack went unanswered, the Fast and Furious gun-running fiasco refused to go away, and revelations of domestic spying by the super-secret National Security Agency shocked many Americans. The Internal Revenue Service acknowledged targeting conservative political groups for special scrutiny, and the government admitted tapping the telephones of the Associated Press. The proliferation of the use of drones by the NSA added to fears of illegal government snooping.

Health and Human Services Secretary Kathleen Sibelius appeared before Congress to defend the disastrous opening of the Affordable Care Act, but satisfactory explanations of its difficulties were hard to come by.

MICHAEL RAMIREZ
Investor's Business Daily

RICK MCKEE
Augusta Chronicle

SCOTT STANTIS
Chicago Tribune

STEVE KELLEY
Creators Syndicate

MICHAEL RAMIREZ
Investor's Business Daily

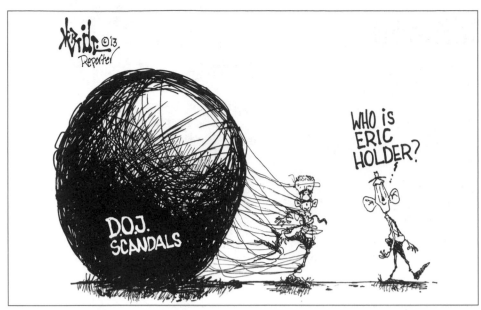

STEVE MCBRIDE
Independence Daily Reporter (Kan.)

MIKE LESTER
Washington Post Writers Group

DANA SUMMERS
Orlando Sentinel

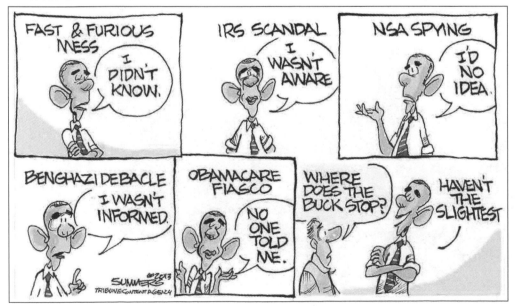

TED RALL
Universal Uclick

TIM EAGAN
timeagan.com

19

LISA BENSON
Washington Post Writers Group

JAKE FULLER
Artizans Syndicate

MIKE LUCKOVICH
Atlanta Journal-Constitution

DAVID HORSEY
Los Angeles Times

JEFF STAHLER
GOCOMICS.COM

DRIVING WHILE BARACK

CLAY BENNETT
Chattanooga Times-Free Press

JOE LICCAR
Examiner-Gatehouse Media

JAKE FULLER
Artizans Syndicate

MARK STREETER
Savannah Morning News

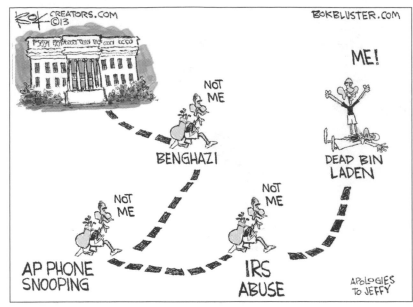

CHIP BOK
Creators.com

NATE BEELER
Columbus Dispatch

PHIL HANDS
Wisconsin State Journal

JOSEPH HOFFECKER
Cincinnati Business Courier

THEO MOUDAKIS
Toronto Star

CHUCK LEGGE
The Frontiersman (Alaska)

CLAY BENNETT
Chattanooga Times-Free Press

LARRY WRIGHT
Caglecartoons.com

THE ARTIST

PLEASE TELL ME YOU'RE EXPECTING A PACKAGE FROM AMAZON...

©2013
BRANCH
BRANCHTOON.COM

Hazardous to Your Wealth

28

Obamacare

Obama's signature achievement, the Affordable Care Act, went into effect Oct. 1. It was a rocky start. The government website was slow and fraught with problems, frequently crashing. People trying to enroll by telephone found that no easier. Relatively few were able to complete the process. By mid-November, the government reported that only about 100,000 had signed up. Millions had been expected.

Obama's oft-repeated promise, "If you like your insurance plan, you can keep it," proved not to be true. Millions of Americans received letters informing them their insurance had been canceled. Many complained that their options were more expensive than insurance they already had and did not offer what they wanted. The president at first claimed that the canceled insurance plans had been replaced because they were substandard, but later acknowledged that was not always the case and apologized.

Democrats up for reelection grew increasingly nervous over the website disaster and asked that implementation be delayed. Young people, deemed essential for success of the program, seemed to be distancing themselves from it.

Dissatisfaction with Obamacare caused the president's approval rating to plummet.

DAVID HITCH
Worcester Telegram & Gazette

STEVE MCBRIDE
Independence Daily Reporter (Kan.)

DEB MILBRATH
debmilbrath@comcast.net

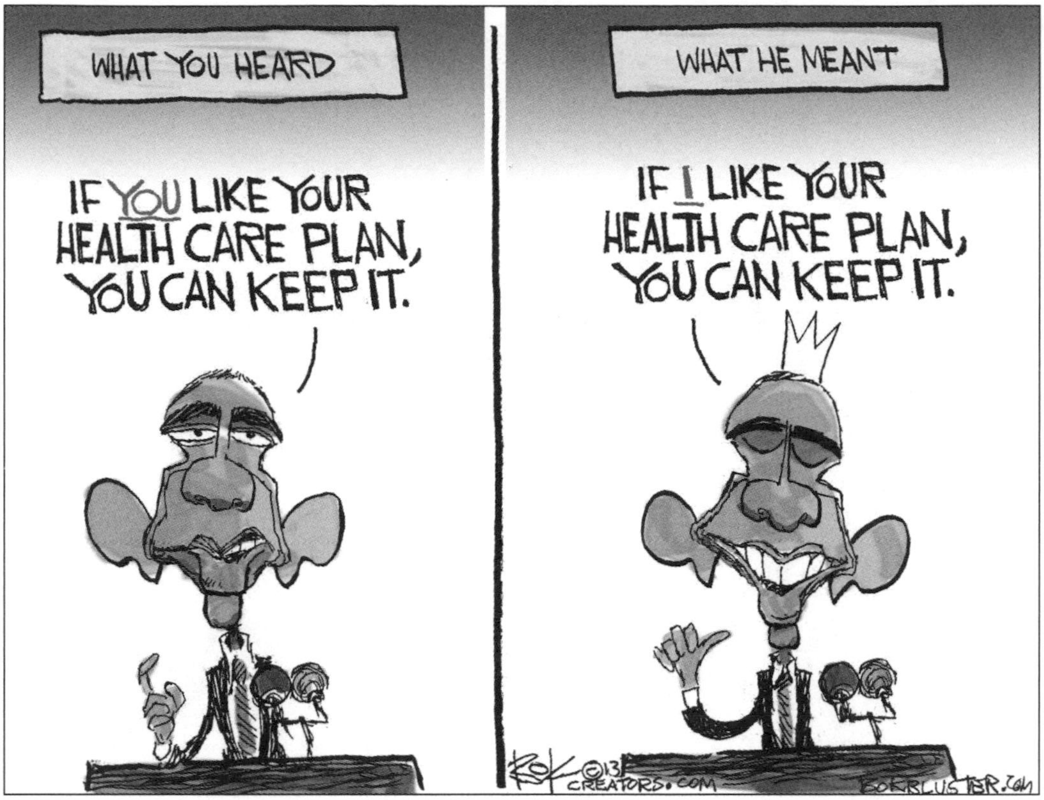
WHAT YOU HEARD
IF YOU LIKE YOUR HEALTH CARE PLAN, YOU CAN KEEP IT.
WHAT HE MEANT
IF I LIKE YOUR HEALTH CARE PLAN, YOU CAN KEEP IT.
BOK ©13 CREATORS.COM

CHIP BOK
Creators.com

STEVE KELLEY
Creators Syndicate

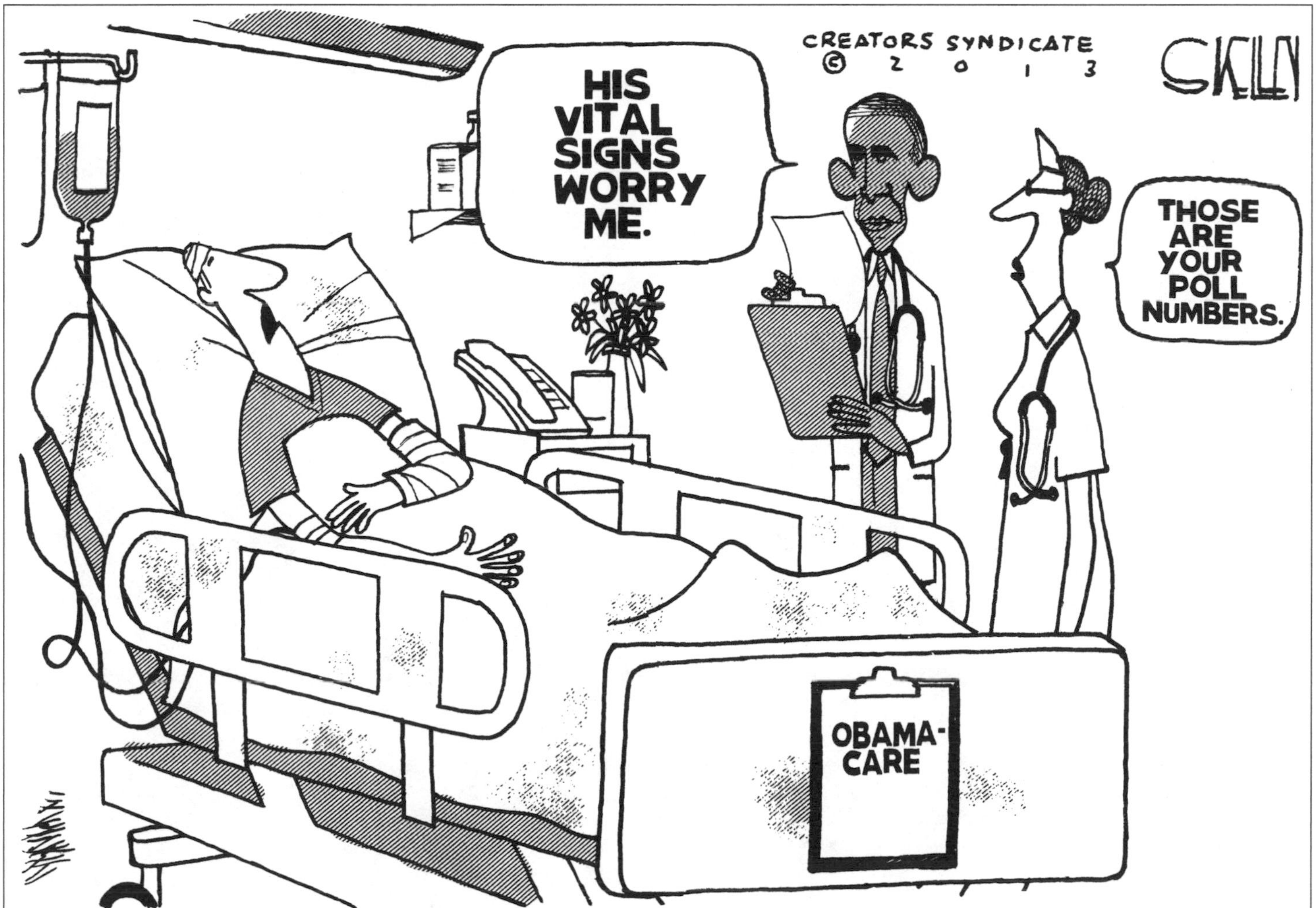
CREATORS SYNDICATE © 2013
KELLEY
HIS VITAL SIGNS WORRY ME.
THOSE ARE YOUR POLL NUMBERS.
OBAMA-CARE

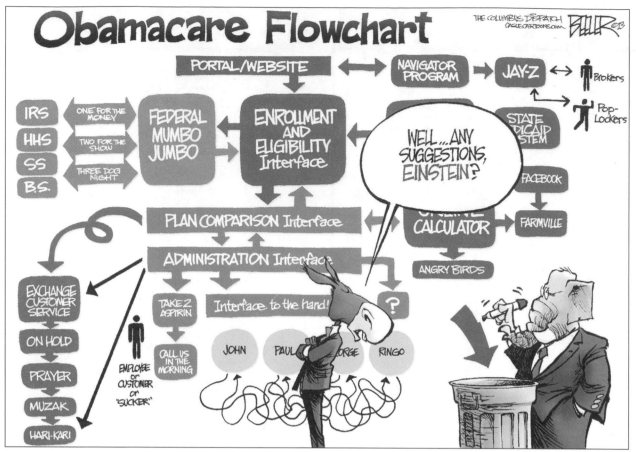

MICHAEL RAMIREZ
Investor's Business Daily

NATE BEELER
Columbus Dispatch

GLENN FODEN
Media Research Center

STEVE SACK
The Star Tribune (Minn.)

MIKE PETERS
Dayton Daily News

CLAY BENNETT
Chattanooga Times-Free Press

'Luckily, mental illness is covered under Obamacare.'

PHIL HANDS
Wisconsin State Journal

ROGER SCHILLERSTROM
Crain Communications

GUS RODRIGUEZ
Garrinchatoons.com

TIM CAMPBELL
Current Publishing

DANA SUMMERS
Orlando Sentinel

MIKE LESTER
Washington Post Writers Group

JOEL PETT
Lexington Herald-Leader

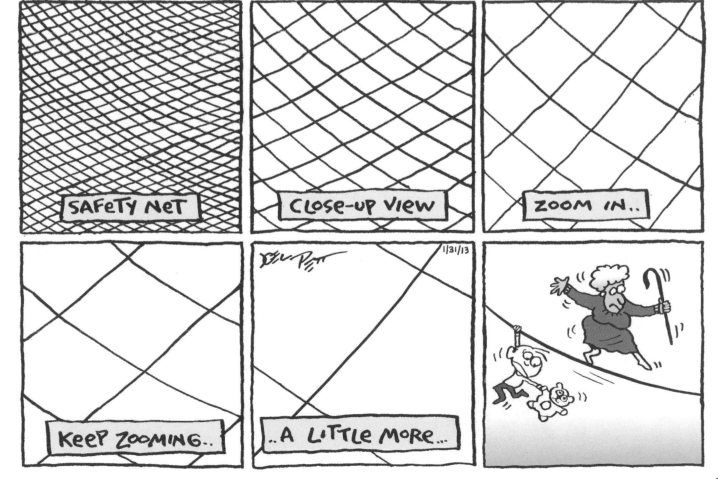

TOM BECK
Shaw Media

ROBERT ARIAIL
Universal Uclick

CHIP BOK
Creators.com

GARY VARVEL
Indianapolis Star

GLENN FODEN
Media Research Center

JESSE SPRINGER
Eugene Register-Guard

STEVE KELLEY
Creators Syndicate

ED GAMBLE
King Features Syndicate

41

MIKE LESTER
Washington Post Writers Group

PAUL BERGE
Q Syndicate

42

Gun Control

Incidents such as the massacre of school children in Newtown, Connecticut, and the killing of a dozen people at the Navy yard in Washington rekindled the debate over gun control. At the same time, gun sales soared. In the U.S. there are roughly 300 million firearms, of which about 100 million are handguns. Handguns are reportedly used in more than 87 percent of violent crimes. Although mass shootings get most of the media attention, they account for only a small percentage of gun deaths. A growing percentage of gun owners cite personal protection as their reason for gun ownership.

In April the Senate turned down a plan to expand background checks on sales of firearms, as well as a proposal to ban semi-automatic weapons and limit the size of clips to ten rounds. Opposition to the plan was led by conservative Republicans and the National Rifle Association. They were joined by some Democrats from pro-gun states.

Although an overwhelming majority of citizens favor background checks, the political climate is not right for major gun control legislation, according to some analysts. Reaction to the not guilty verdict in a highly publicized shooting case in Florida continued throughout the year.

CLAY BENNETT
Chattanooga Times-Free Press

LYNN CARLSON and BILL SMITH
Lompoc Record

MIKE BECKOM
Index-Journal (Ind.)

TIM JACKSON
Freelance

CAGLECARTOONS.COM
GARY@GARYMCCOY.ORG

ZIMMERMAN:
NOT
GUILTY!

GARY MCCOY
Caglecartoons.com

BOB GORRELL
Creators Syndicate

©2013 CREATORS.COM
GORRELLART.COM
GORREL

AND PEOPLE
WONDER WHY
JUSTICE IS GIVEN A
BLINDFOLD...

MEDIA CRITICISM

RACIAL BACKLASH

ZIMMERMAN
VERDICT

MIKE SMITH
Las Vegas Sun

THEO MOUDAKIS
Toronto Star

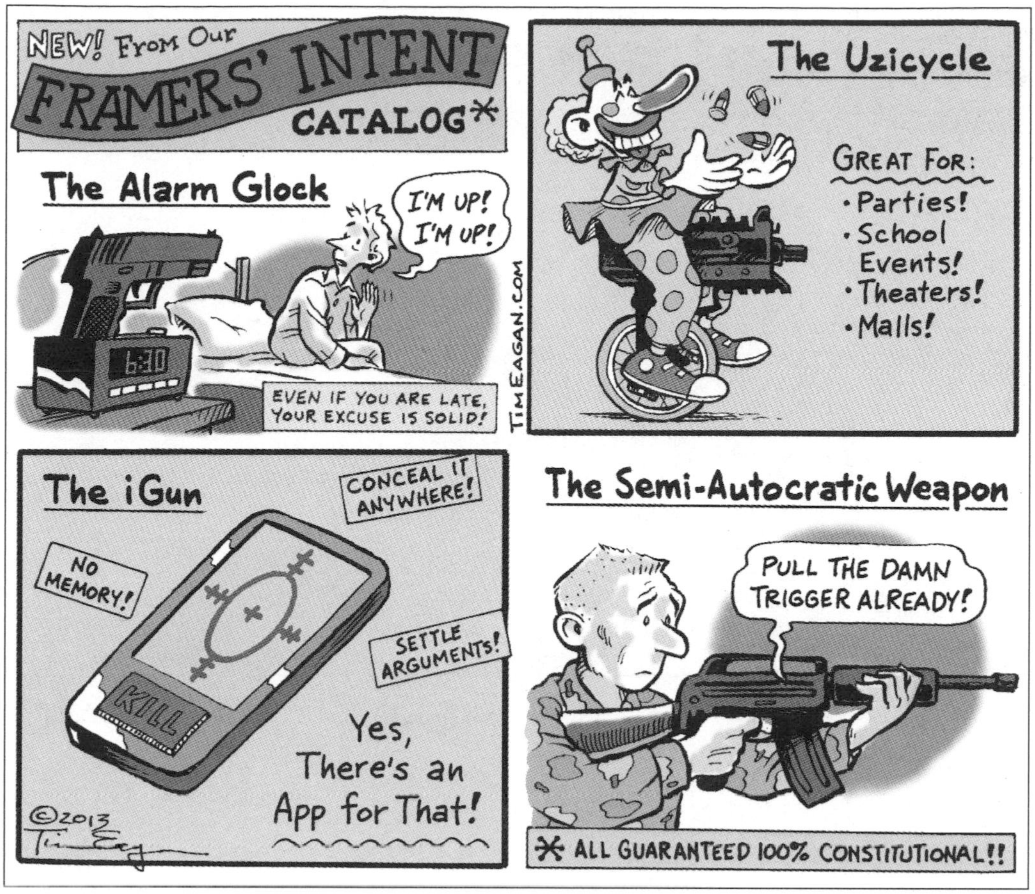
NEW! From Our
FRAMERS' INTENT
CATALOG*
The Alarm Glock
I'M UP! I'M UP!
6:30
EVEN IF YOU ARE LATE, YOUR EXCUSE IS SOLID!
TIMEAGAN.COM
The Uzicycle
GREAT FOR:
• Parties!
• School Events!
• Theaters!
• Malls!
The iGun
CONCEAL IT ANYWHERE!
NO MEMORY!
SETTLE ARGUMENTS!
KILL
Yes, There's an App for That!
©2013
The Semi-Autocratic Weapon
PULL THE DAMN TRIGGER ALREADY!
* ALL GUARANTEED 100% CONSTITUTIONAL!!

TIM EAGAN
timeagan.com

MIKE LUCKOVICH
Atlanta Journal-Constitution

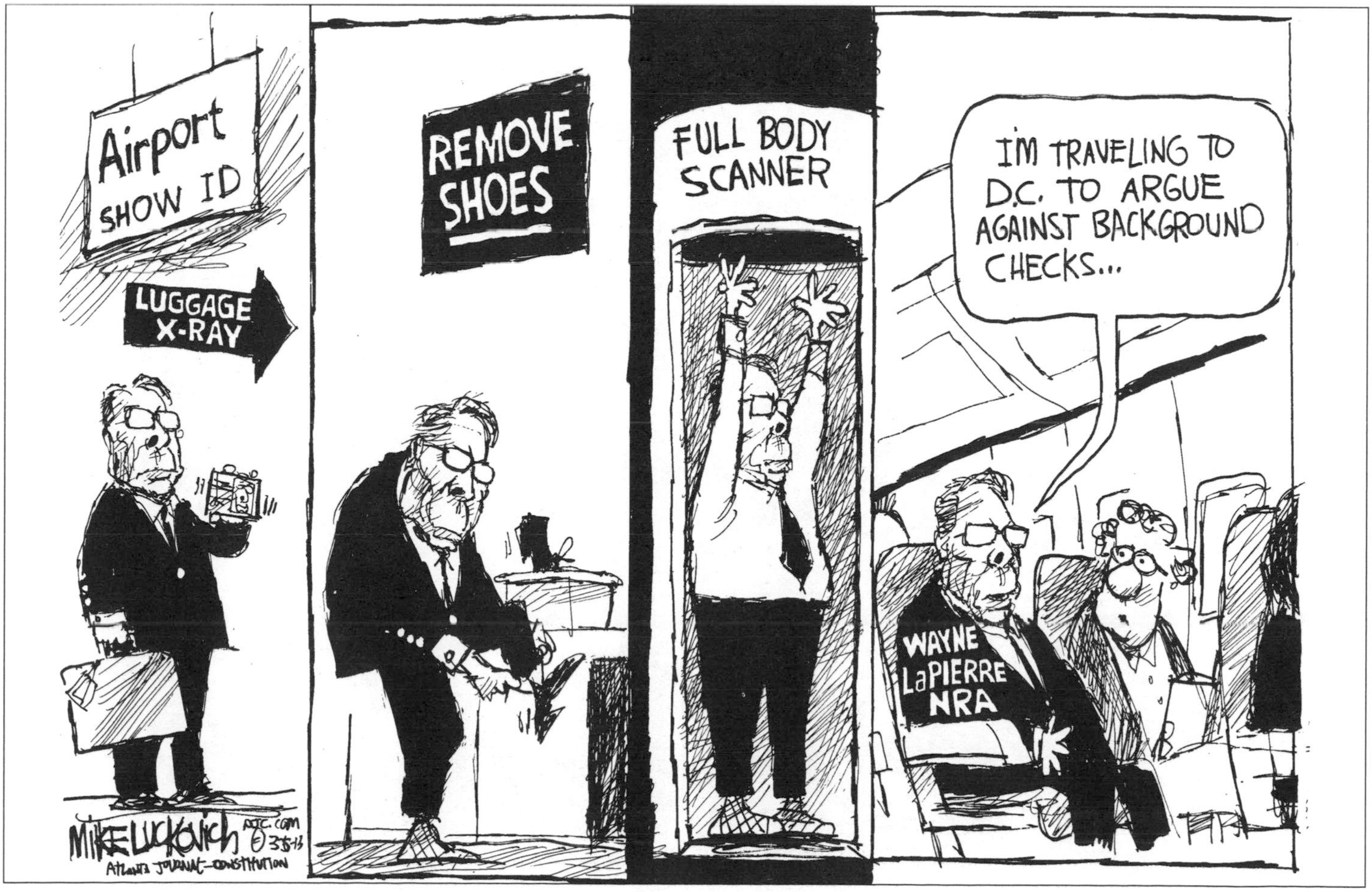
Airport
SHOW ID
LUGGAGE X-RAY
REMOVE SHOES
FULL BODY SCANNER
I'M TRAVELING TO D.C. TO ARGUE AGAINST BACKGROUND CHECKS...
WAYNE LaPIERRE NRA
MIKE LUCKOVICH
ATLANTA JOURNAL-CONSTITUTION

CHARLES DANIEL
Knoxville News-Sentinel

DAVID BROWN
David Brown Studios

WILLIAM FLINT
Dallas Morning News

MIKE LESTER
Washington Post Writers Group

DOUG MACGREGOR
Fort Myers News-Press

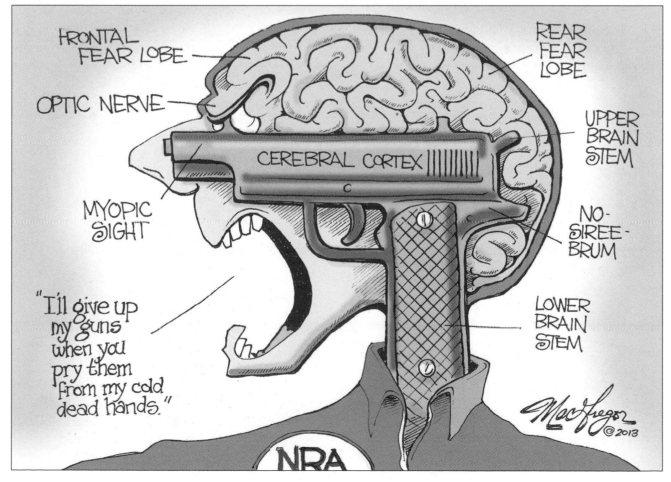

JESSE SPRINGER
Eugene Register-Guard

PAUL BERGE
Q Syndicate

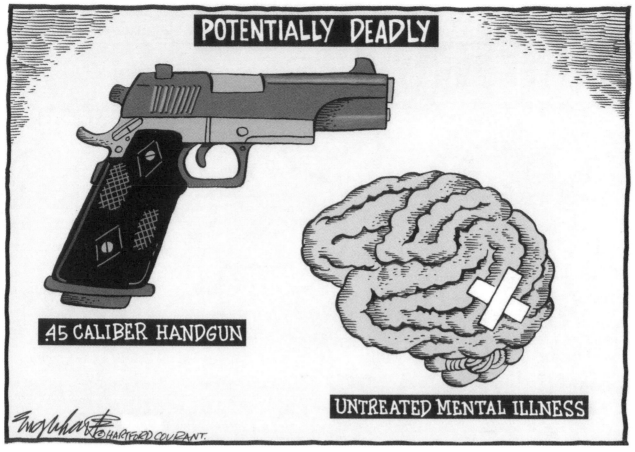

BOB ENGLEHART
Caglecartoons.com

MIKE MARLAND
Concord Monitor

RUSSELL HODIN
New Times (Calif.)

RUSSELL HODIN
New Times (Calif.)

DANA SUMMERS
Orlando Sentinel

PAUL FELL
Artizans Syndicate

BRUCE PLANTE
Tulsa World Media Co.

53

KATE SALLEY PALMER
Artizans.com

JEFF BOYER
Albany Times-Union

Gay Marriage

The Supreme Court struck down a key provision of the federal Defense of Marriage Act, declaring that same-sex couples who are legally married have the same rights under the federal law as all other married couples. The ruling did not affect the portion of the law that allows states to make their own determinations on marriage policy. The decision was seen as a major victory for gay rights, and possibly a tipping point in the court of public opinion. It will likely give renewed impetus to challenges of state bans against same-sex marriage.

At least 32 states still have laws banning same-sex unions. In the past year, Illinois, New Mexico, Hawaii, New Jersey, Minnesota, Delaware, Rhode Island, Colorado, and Maryland became the latest states to approve. It is estimated that there are more than half a million gay couples in the U.S.

Indiana and Utah have become battleground states in the national dispute over gay marriage. Indiana lawmakers plan to put a measure before the voters banning gay marriage, while in Utah, the governor announced the state would not recognize same-sex marriages. A federal judge in Ohio ruled that the state must recognize gay marriages on death certificates.

ROGER SCHILLERSTROM
Crain Communications

MIKE LUCKOVICH
Atlanta Journal-Constitution

J.D. CROWE
Mobile Press-Register

56

NATE BEELER
Columbus Dispatch

PAUL BERGE
Q Syndicate

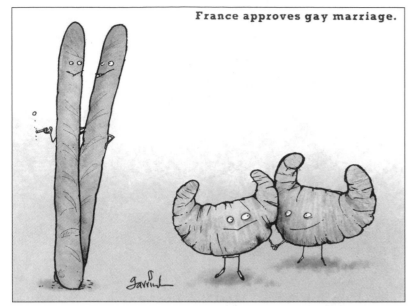

GUS RODRIGUEZ
Garrinchatoons.com

PHIL HANDS
Wisconsin State Journal

JEFF BOYER
Albany Times-Union

MIKE LUCKOVICH
Atlanta Journal-Constitution

BRUCE PLANTE
Tulsa World Media Co.

MIKE SMITH
Las Vegas Sun

DAVID HORSEY
Los Angeles Times

CHAN LOWE
South Florida Sun-Sentinel

JIM DYKE
News-Tribune (Mo.)

Immigration

According to polls, immigration reform and gun control are the bottom two concerns of the American people, on a list of twelve issues facing the nation. Those polls seem to be borne out in Congress, where little has been accomplished on either front.

Immigration reform advocates had a frustrating year. A diverse coalition of business, faith, and civil rights leaders supported legislation to reform the nation's immigration laws. After thousands of demonstrators descended on Washington to attend a National Rally for Citizenship, a bipartisan group of senators called the Gang of Eight introduced a bill that would provide a path to citizenship for illegal immigrants. The bill passed the Senate, but stalled in the House. More deportations have occurred under the Obama administration than under any other president.

Activists also lobbied for immigration reform with prayer vigils, marches, and civil disobedience, including blocking buses deporting illegal immigrants and shutting down congressional offices with sit-ins. Polls show a majority of Americans support a way to gain citizenship for the estimated 11 million undocumented aliens in the country. Analysts say passage of a comprehensive immigration reform bill is a real possibility in 2014.

CHUCK ASAY
Creators Syndicate

DAVID FITZSIMMONS
The Arizona Star

JIMMY MARGULIES
The Record (N.J.)

WILLIAM FLINT
Dallas Morning News

GUS RODRIGUEZ
Garrinchatoons.com

GARY MCCOY
Caglecartoons.com

ROB ROGERS
Pittsburgh Post-Gazette

GARY VARVEL
Indianapolis Star

JIM MORIN
Miami Herald

CHUCK LEGGE
The Frontiersman (Alaska)

MARC MURPHY
The Courier-Journal (Ky.)

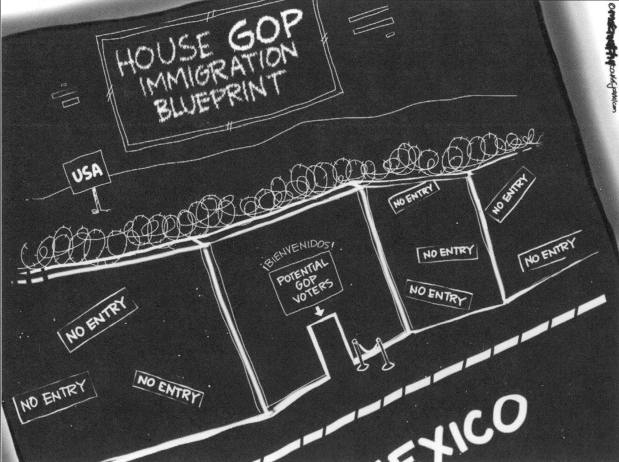

Congress

Gridlock caused Congress to record one of the least productive sessions in years, although some said that might be a good thing. The government shutdown over Obamacare was symptomatic of Congress' inability to agree on a direction for the nation. As a result, the public's opinion of Congress fell to a new low. Late in the year, polls showed only 10 percent approved of congressional actions. Nevertheless, the President saw fit to grant Congress a waiver on the new health care program.

Sen. Ted Cruz delivered a 21-hour, 19-minute speech, one of the longest in Senate history, in opposition to the Affordable Care Act. Such speeches, along with Senate inaction on Obama appointees, led frustrated Democrats to trigger the "Nuclear Option," which weakened the power of the filibuster. In a 52-48 vote, the Democrat-controlled Senate changed a longstanding rule for cutting off filibusters. A filibuster can now be stopped with only a simple majority—not the previously required 60 votes. The change does not apply to Supreme Court nominees or legislation.

TIM HARTMAN
timhartman.com

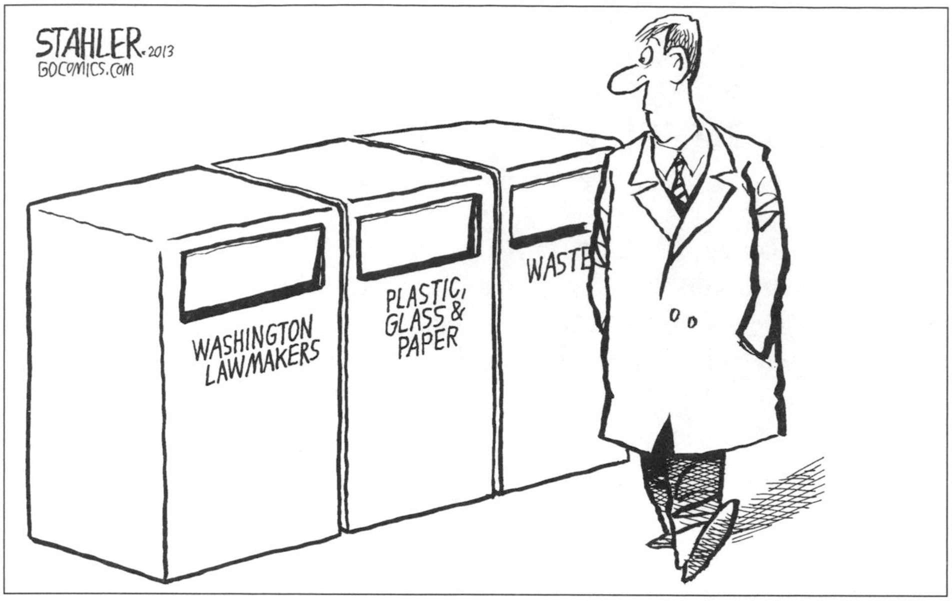
STAHLER © 2013
GOCOMICS.com
WASHINGTON LAWMAKERS
PLASTIC, GLASS & PAPER
WASTE

JEFF STAHLER
GOCOMICS.COM

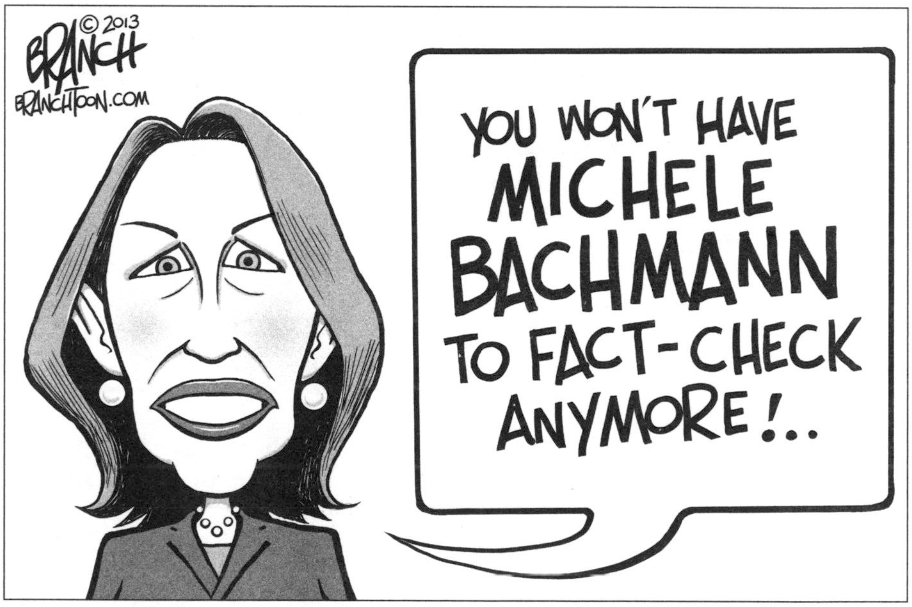
© 2013
BRANCH
BRANCHTOON.COM
YOU WON'T HAVE MICHELE BACHMANN TO FACT-CHECK ANYMORE!..

JOHN BRANCH
Branchtoon.com

DANIEL FENECH
Saline Reporter (Mich.)

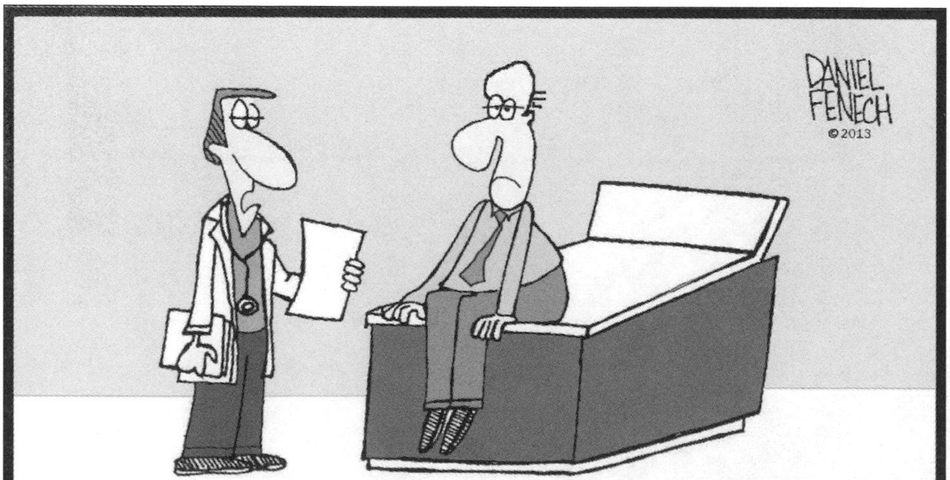
DANIEL FENECH
©2013
"I'VE SEEN THIS SAME AFFLICTION IN OTHER CONGRESSMEN. YOU HAVE NEGOTIATION-DEFICIT DISORDER."

ED HALL
Artizans.com

TIM HARTMAN
timhartman.com

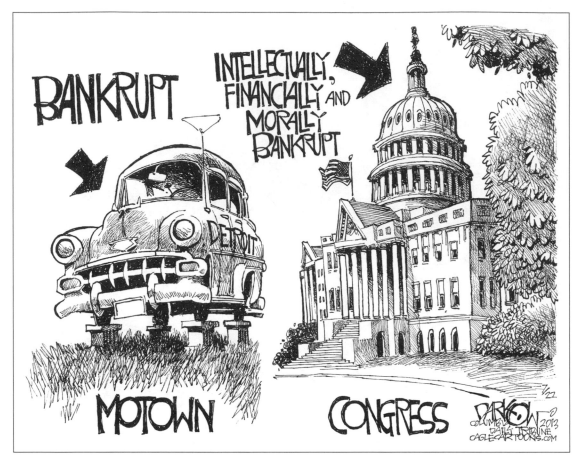

JOHN DARKOW
Columbia Daily Tribune (Mo.)

ED GAMBLE
King Features Syndicate

DEB MILBRATH
debmilbrath@comcast.net

WAYNE STROOT
Hastings Tribune

MIKE MARLAND
Concord Monitor

CHAN LOWE
South Florida Sun-Sentinel

CHRIS WEYANT
The Hill

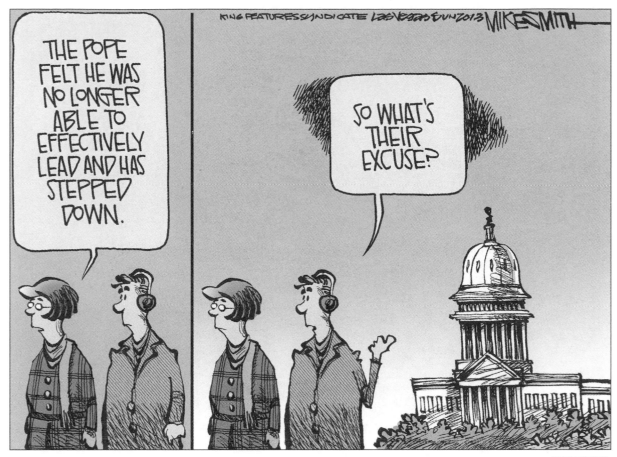

MIKE SMITH
Las Vegas Sun

R.J. MATSON
Roll Call

STEVE KELLEY
Creators Syndicate

JIMMY MARGULIES
The Record (N.J.)

Reaching Across the Aisle...

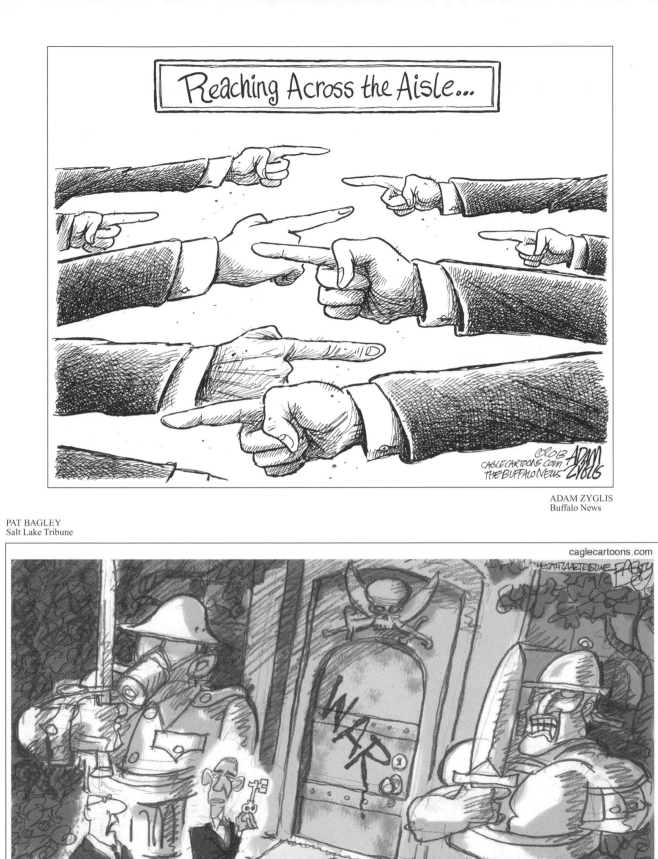

ADAM ZYGLIS
Buffalo News

PAT BAGLEY
Salt Lake Tribune

"TECHNICALLY, YOU MAY NEED TO ASK THE DOORMAT'S PERMISSION"

THE BOSTON MARATHON

S.W. PARRA
Fresno Bee

TOM STIGLICH
Creators Syndicate

Senseless.

Crime / Terrorism

A twenty-year-old fatally shot twenty children and six adult staff members at Sandy Hook Elementary School in Newtown, Connecticut. Before driving to the school, the young man killed his mother. He then shot himself in the head as responders arrived.

It was the second deadliest mass shooting by a single person in American history, after the 2007 Virginia Tech massacre. The incident prompted renewed debate over gun control. Audio recordings of 911 calls related to the incidents were released in December.

Near the finish line of the Boston Marathon, two bombs were set off, killing 3 people and injuring 264 others. The Federal Bureau of Investigation identified two suspects, brothers Dzhokhar and Tamerlan Tsarnaev. The suspects later allegedly killed a police officer, carjacked an SUV, and initiated an exchange of gunfire with police. Tamerlan Tsarnaev was run over by his brother Dzhokhar, and Dzhokhar Tsarnaev was injured. He was captured after an unprecedented manhunt by thousands of law enforcement officers. Dzhokhar was arrested and charged with use of a weapon of mass destruction and malicious destruction of property resulting in death. He pleaded not guilty to thirty charges.

MARC MURPHY
The Courier-Journal (Ky.)

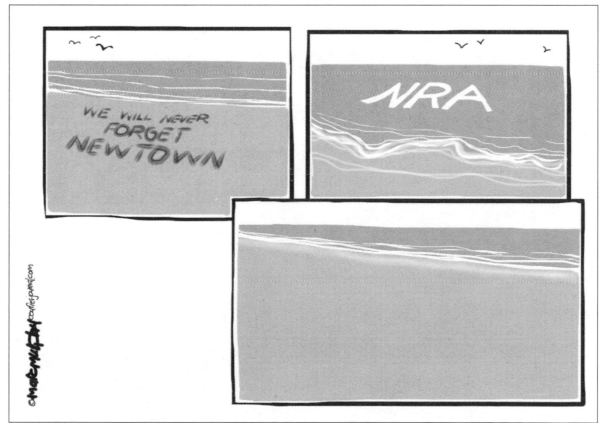

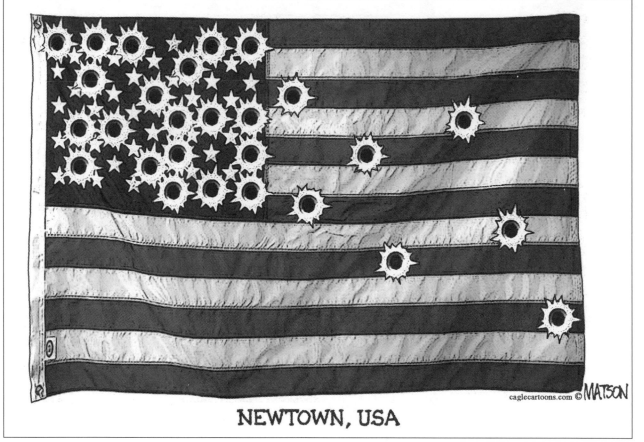

NEWTOWN, USA

R.J. MATSON
Roll Call

KEVIN KALLAUGHER
Baltimore Sun

JEFF DARCY
The Plain Dealer (Oh.)

MIKE PETERS
Dayton Daily News

ALWAYS REMEMBER TO THANK A TEACHER.

CHAN LOWE
South Florida Sun-Sentinel

BILL DAY
Caglecartoons.com

Little Johnny Gets Dressed for School

Socks

Underwear

Belt

T-Shirt

Jacket

Shirt

Blue Jeans

Sneakers

NATIONAL RIFLE ASSOCIATION

Bullet-Proof Vest

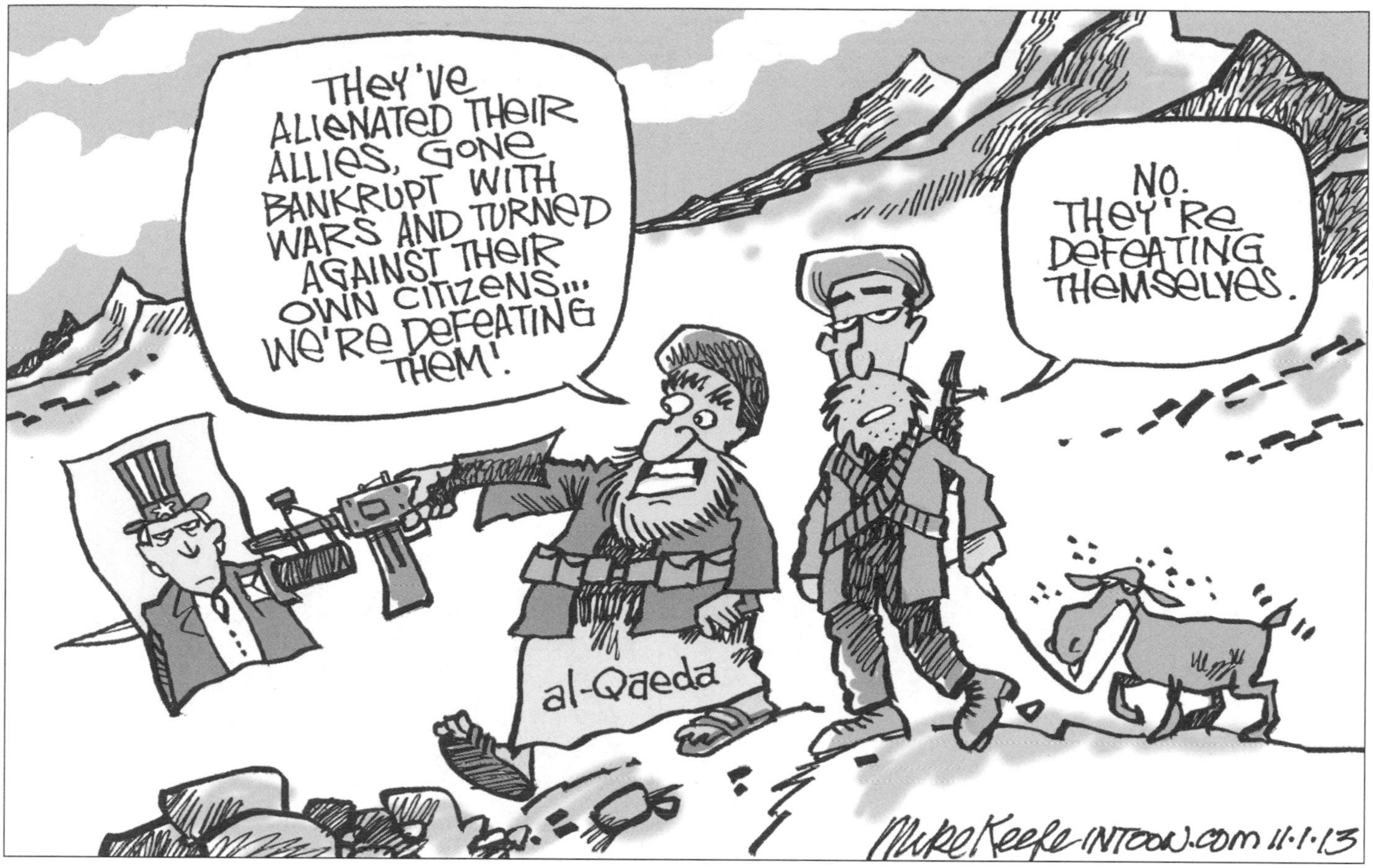
THEY'VE ALIENATED THEIR ALLIES, GONE BANKRUPT WITH WARS AND TURNED AGAINST THEIR OWN CITIZENS... WE'RE DEFEATING THEM!
al-Qaeda
NO. THEY'RE DEFEATING THEMSELVES.
MIKE KEEFE - INTOON.COM 11.1.13

MIKE KEEFE
Caglecartoons.com

MONTE WOLVERTON
Caglecartoons.com

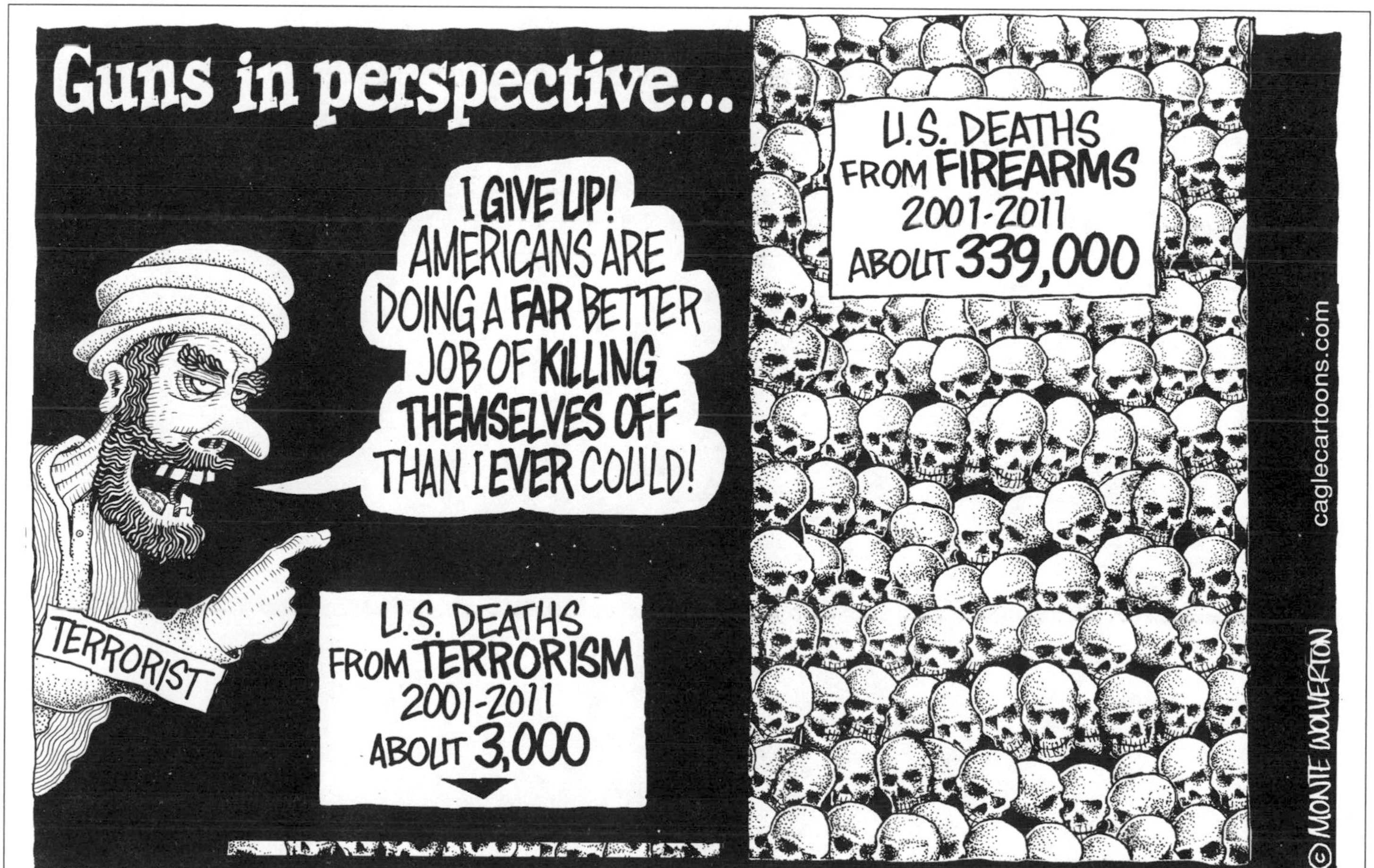
Guns in perspective...
I GIVE UP! AMERICANS ARE DOING A FAR BETTER JOB OF KILLING THEMSELVES OFF THAN I EVER COULD!
TERRORIST
U.S. DEATHS FROM TERRORISM 2001-2011 ABOUT 3,000
U.S. DEATHS FROM FIREARMS 2001-2011 ABOUT 339,000
caglecartoons.com
© MONTE WOLVERTON

STEVE BREEN
San Diego Union-Tribune

GARY MCCOY
Caglecartoons.com

84

Government Shutdown

Automatic spending cuts, known as sequestration, went into effect in 2013 as the result of a congressional attempt to curb the mushrooming federal deficit. The GOP-led House in September passed a continuing resolution to fund the government but eliminate Obamacare. Sen. Ted Cruz gave a lengthy speech attacking the health plan. After the Senate rejected the House bill, the GOP modified its demands, seeking a one-year delay in implementation. Obama refused to negotiate "with a gun to my head."

That led to a partial government shutdown on Oct. 1. Government workers were furloughed. The WWII memorial in Washington was closed, shutting out veterans. National parks were padlocked. Survivors of soldiers killed in Afghanistan were denied survivor benefits and transportation to greet returning coffins.

The House attempted to pass popular federal programs one by one, but the Democrat-led Senate rejected this "piecemeal" funding of the government. Hoping to head off another government shutdown, the House passed a modest budget deal in mid-December.

Polls show most people tended to blame Republicans for the shutdown.

BRUCE MACKINNON
Halifax Herald (Can.)

JAKE FULLER
Artizans Syndicate

CHRIS BRITT
State-Journal Register (Ill.)

GEORGE DANBY
Bangor Daily News (Me.)

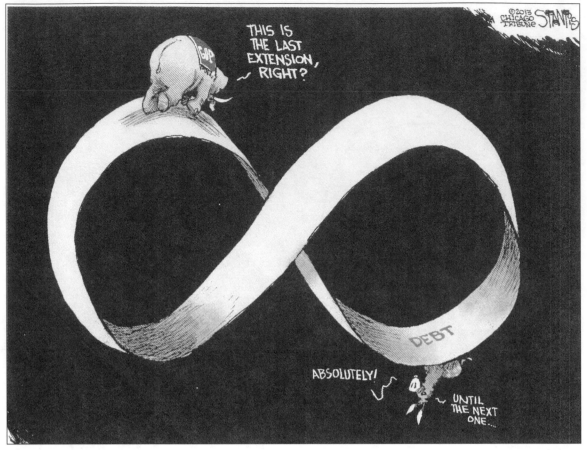

SCOTT STANTIS
Chicago Tribune

TONY BAYER
Tonybayertoons.com

STEVE KELLEY
Creators Syndicate

STEVE SACK
The Star Tribune (Minn.)

89

STEVE MCBRIDE
Independence Daily Reporter (Kan.)

Budget cuts cause shutdown of contol towers at small airports across the country.

NEIL GRAHAME
Spencer Newspapers

TOM STIGLICH
Creators Syndicate

CHRIS WEYANT
The Hill

STEVE SACK
The Star Tribune (Minn.)

JEFF PARKER
Parkertoons

LISA BENSON
Washington Post Writers Group

PHIL HANDS
Wisconsin State Journal

RICK MCKEE
Augusta Chronicle

JEFF DARCY
The Plain Dealer (Oh.)

TIM BENSON
Sioux Falls Argus-Leader (S.D.)

DARYL CAGLE
Caglecartoons.com

MATT WUERKER
Politico

TOM BECK
Shaw Media

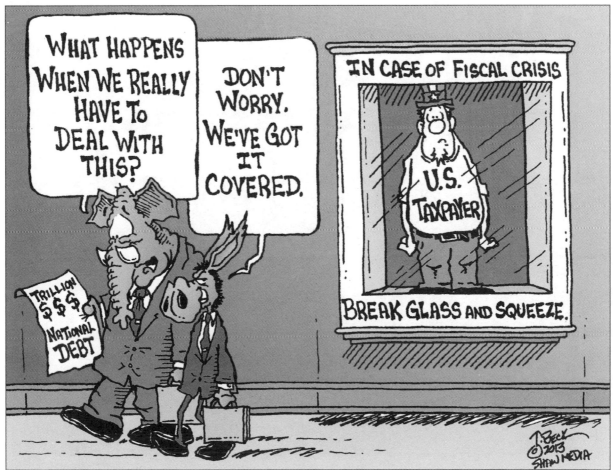

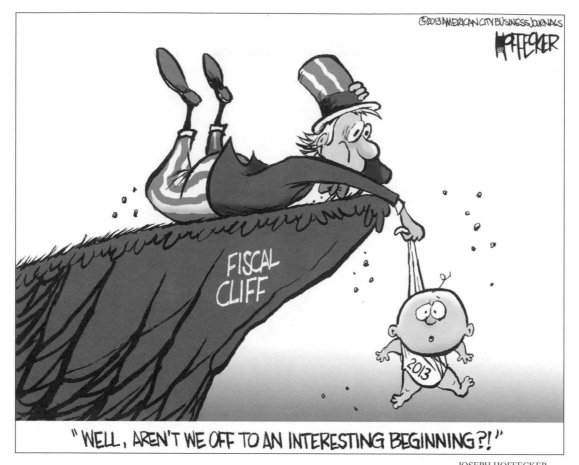

JOSEPH HOFFECKER
Cincinnati Business Courier

JEFF PARKER
Parkertoons

RUSSELL HODIN
New Times (Calif.)

JOHN BRANCH
Branchtoon.com

MIKE KEEFE
Caglecartoons.com

AL GOODWYN
Courtesy Al Goodwyn

NATE BEELER
Columbus Dispatch

The Economy

The Federal Reserve began winding down the era of easy money in late 2013, pronouncing the U.S. economy strong enough to cut back on its massive bond-buying stimulus. The central bank modestly trimmed the pace of monthly asset purchases from $85 billion to $75 billion. At the same time, the Fed sought to reassure financial markets, suggesting that the key interest rate would remain low.

Investors seemed to take the move as validation that the economy was improving. The slow recovery caused businesses to be wary of spending, keeping margins high. The surprising result: Despite a poor economy, the stock market was performing well. At the same time, however, personal income was down sharply. In 2013 poverty among children reached record levels, with 16.7 million youths living in food-insecure households. More than 10 million people were added to the food stamp program in the last four years, an increase of 26 percent.

U.S. job growth slowed in October as a partial shutdown of the government delayed hiring and forced some workers to stay home, undermining the economy's fourth-quarter growth prospects. The unemployment rate rose slightly to 7.3 percent.

CHRIS BRITT
State-Journal Register (Ill.)

WILLIAM FLINT
Dallas Morning News

CHARLES BEYL
Lancaster Sunday News (Pa.)

MIKE KEEFE
Caglecartoons.com

UNEMPLOYMENT

RICK KOLLINGER
Star-Democrat (Md.)

GEORGE DANBY
Bangor Daily News (Me.)

CHUCK LEGGE
The Frontiersman (Alaska)

GLENN FODEN
Media Research Center

MATT BORS
Medium

JIMMY MARGULIES
The Record (N.J.)

ED GAMBLE
King Features Syndicate

TOM BECK
Shaw Media

ROGER SCHILLERSTROM
Crain Communications

ANNETTE BALESTERI
Antioch News (Calif.)

STEVE LINDSTROM
Duluth News-Tribune

TIM CAMPBELL
Current Publishing

LARRY WRIGHT
Caglecartoons.com

ROB ROGERS
Pittsburgh Post-Gazette

KEVIN KALLAUGHER
Baltimore Sun

HIS RED LINES

RANAN LURIE
Lurie Studios

Foreign Affairs

Six nations, including the United States, reached "an initial agreement" with Iran regarding its nuclear program. Under the tentative arrangement, Iran would promise to scale back its nuclear activities in exchange for the lifting of certain economic sanctions. Negotiations toward a full agreement were expected within a year.

President Obama threatened action against Syria after Bashar al-Assad's government used chemical weapons against Syrian rebel forces. Obama established figurative red lines in the dust but did nothing when the lines were crossed. Vladimir Putin, lately a thorn in the side regarding U.S. interests, opposed action against Syria and apparently persuaded Assad to surrender his chemical stockpiles.

Putin earlier in the year had tweaked the U.S. when he provided refuge for Edward Snowden, the rogue National Security Agency contractor who was accused of stealing tens of thousands of top secret U.S. documents.

North Korea continued to agitate under the leadership of its erratic young leader. In Egypt President Mohammed Morsi was deposed in a military coup, leading to widespread violence. Toronto mayor Rob Ford was seen on a video apparently smoking crack. He also admitted to "drunken stupors."

GARY VARVEL
Indianapolis Star

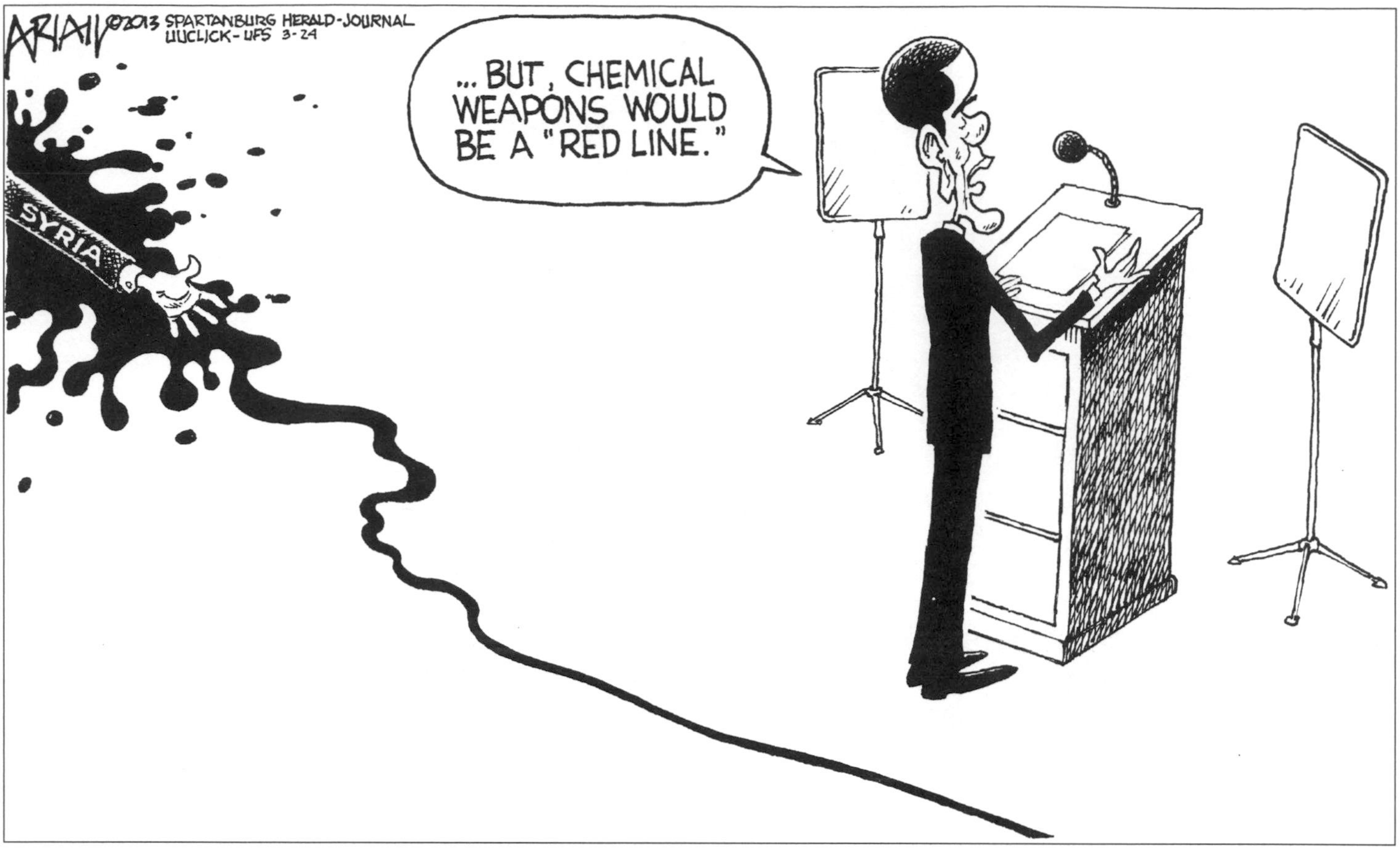
ARIAIL ©2013 SPARTANBURG HERALD-JOURNAL
UUCLICK-UFS 3-24
... BUT, CHEMICAL WEAPONS WOULD BE A "RED LINE."
SYRIA

ROBERT ARIAIL
Universal Uclick

LISA BENSON
Washington Post Writers Group

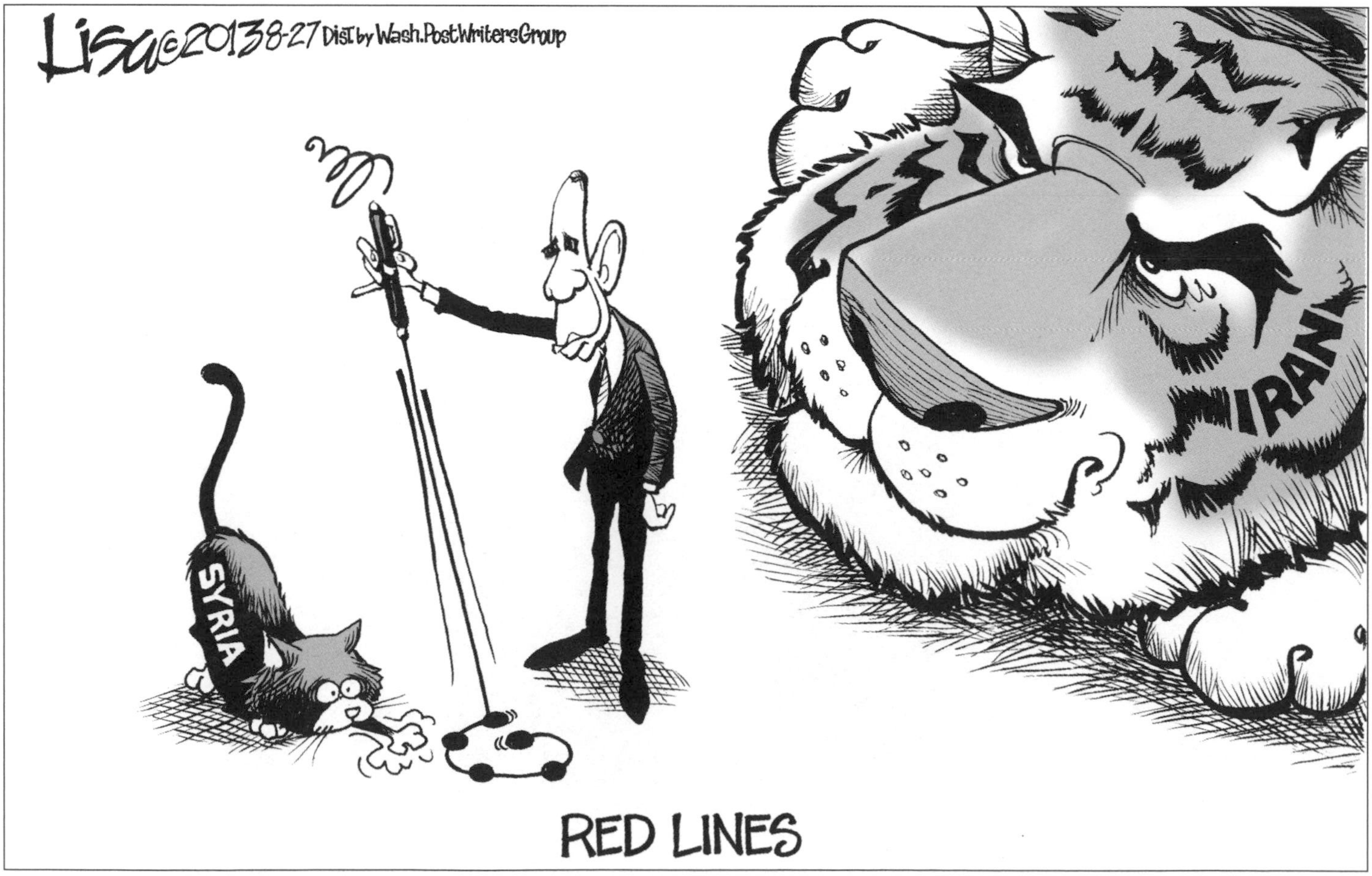
Lisa ©2013 8-27 Dist. by Wash. Post Writers Group
SYRIA
IRAN
RED LINES

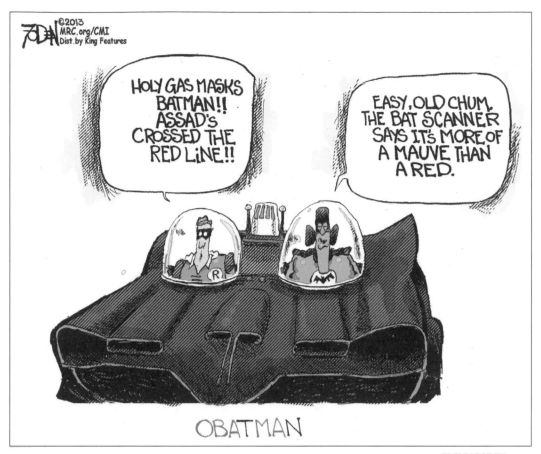

GLENN FODEN
Media Research Center

THEO MOUDAKIS
Toronto Star

MIKE BECKOM
Index-Journal (Ind.)

KAP CAPDEVILA
Caglecartoons.com

BOB ENGLEHART
Caglecartoons.com

TIM CAMPBELL
Current Publishing

MATT BORS
Medium

ERIC ALLIE
Caglecartoons.com

MATT WUERKER
Politico

DARYL CAGLE
Caglecartoons.com

GEORGE DANBY
Bangor Daily News (Me.)

BRUCE MACKINNON
Halifax Herald (Can.)

ROB ROGERS
Pittsburgh Post-Gazette

PETAR PISMETROVIC
Caglecartoons.com

JAKE FULLER
Artizans Syndicate

THEO MOUDAKIS
Toronto Star

BRUCE MACKINNON
Halifax Herald (Can.)

STEVE NEASE
neasecartoons

118

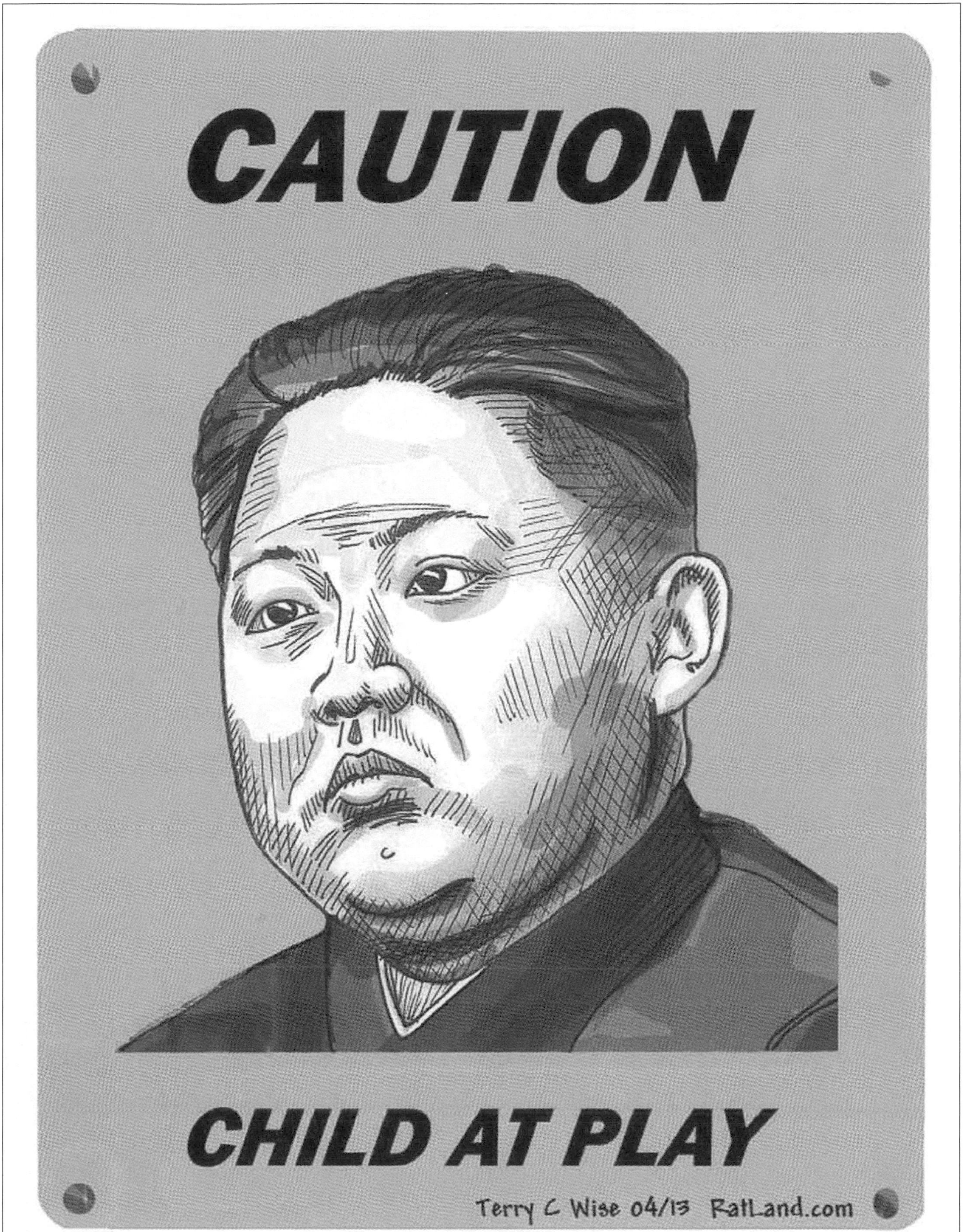
CAUTION
CHILD AT PLAY
Terry C Wise 04/13 RatLand.com

TERRY WISE
ratland.com

ADAM ZYGLIS
Buffalo News

LUOJIE
Caglecartoons.com

CHUCK ASAY
Creators Syndicate

PEDRO X. MOLINA
Confidencial.com.ni

121

TIM HARTMAN
timhartman.com

MICHAEL RAMIREZ
Investor's Business Daily

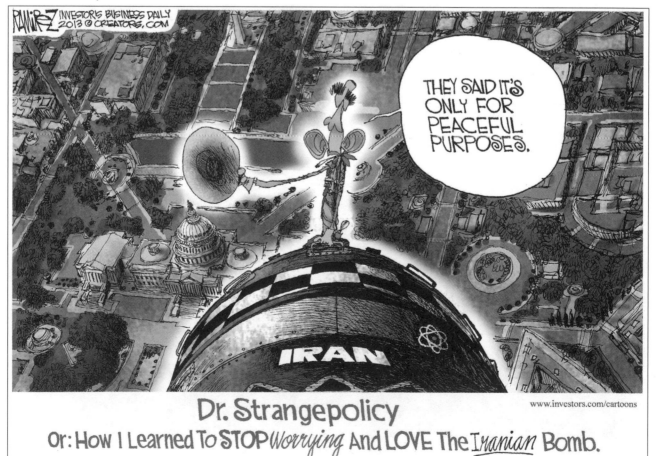

KEVIN KALLAUGHER
The Economist

MIKE KEEFE
Caglecartoons.com

123

RANDY BISH
Tribune-Review (Pa.)

PAUL COMBS
Tribune Content Agency

STEVE MCBRIDE
Independence Daily Reporter (Kan.)

TAYLOR JONES
Caglecartoons.com

©Taylor Jones - Hoover Digest.

caglecartoons.com

ED GAMBLE
King Features Syndicate

JIM MORIN
Miami Herald

Nelson Mandela

Nelson Mandela, the anti-apartheid activist who led South Africa out of oppression, died in December at the age of 95. He was South Africa's first democratically elected leader, serving as president from 1994 to1999.

An African nationalist and democratic socialist, he fought institutionalized racism, poverty, and inequality. Although initially committed to non-violent protest, Mandela co-founded a militant group dedicated to sabotaging the apartheid government. He was arrested, charged with conspiracy to overthrow the government, and sentenced to life in prison. He served twenty-seven years while an international campaign lobbied for his freedom.

He was released in 1990, during a period of escalating civil strife. Mandela negotiated with President F.W. de Klerk to abolish apartheid and hold free elections. As president he helped write a new constitution and formed a commission to investigate past human rights abuse. His administration pushed for land reform, fought poverty, and expanded health care. He declined to run for reelection and became an elder statesman, focusing his efforts on reducing poverty and combating the spread of AIDS.

In his lifetime he received more than 250 honors, including the 1993 Nobel Peace Prize.

MIKE PETERS
Dayton Daily News

TAYLOR JONES
Caglecartoons.com

J.D. CROWE
Mobile Press-Register

MIKE LUCKOVICH
Atlanta Journal-Constitution

STILL UNITING SOUTH AFRICANS

Politics

President Obama's handling of the Affordable Care Act was perhaps the biggest political blunder of 2013. After promising over and over again "If you like your plan, you can keep it," he tried to rewrite that promise after millions of citizens received notices of canceled insurance. That left a lot of people unhappy.

A November CNN/ORC International poll showed a dramatic turnaround in the battle for control of Congress. In October, after the government shutdown, Democrats held a 50 percent to 42 percent advantage. The later poll, taken after the disastrous introduction of Obamacare, showed the GOP with a 49-47 percent edge.

The Tea Party was defeated in a couple of elections, leading a number of pundits to predict its impending demise. Some Tea Party supporters viewed Republican Speaker of the House John Boehner as a bit too liberal.

Possible GOP candidates for the 2016 presidential race appeared to be Gov. Chris Christie, Sen. Ted Cruz, Sen. Rand Paul, and Sen. Marco Rubio. Hillary Clinton was seen by many as having a lock on the Democratic nomination.

CHUCK LEGGE
The Frontiersman (Alaska)

Republican Outreach

CLAY BENNETT
Chattanooga Times-Free Press

DANA SUMMERS
Orlando Sentinel

GRAVITY: THE STORY OF A COUPLE FLOATING AIMLESSLY IN SPACE.

ERIC ALLIE
Caglecartoons.com

GARY VARVEL
Indianapolis Star

131

JEFF STAHLER
GOCOMICS.COM

MARC MURPHY
The Courier-Journal (Ky.)

ROBERT ARIAIL
Universal Uclick

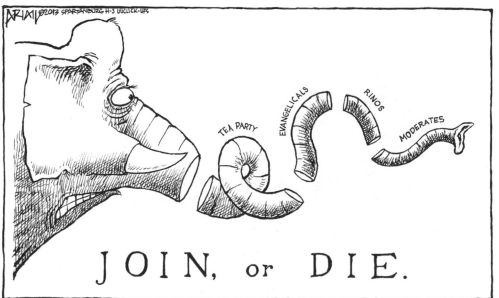

JOHN DARKOW
Columbia Daily Tribune (Mo.)

CHRIS WEYANT
The Hill

PAUL FELL
Artizans Syndicate

MARC MURPHY
The Courier-Journal (Ky.)

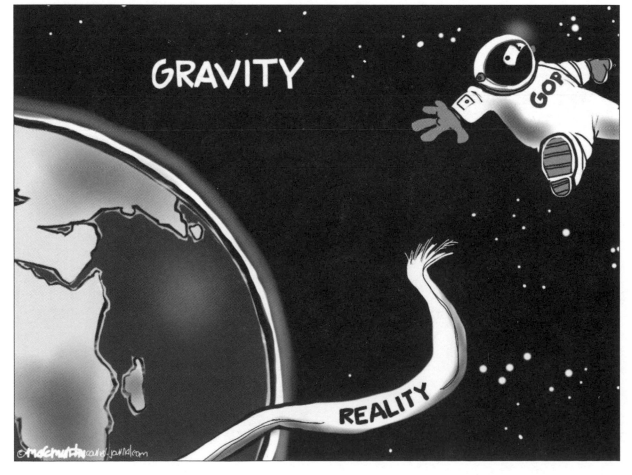

DOUG MACGREGOR
Fort Myers News-Press

NICK ANDERSON
Houston Chronicle

135

STEVE LINDSTROM
Duluth News-Tribune

DARYL CAGLE
Caglecartoons.com

TERRY WISE
ratland.com

ROB ROGERS
Pittsburgh Post-Gazette

DOUG MACGREGOR
Fort Myers News-Press

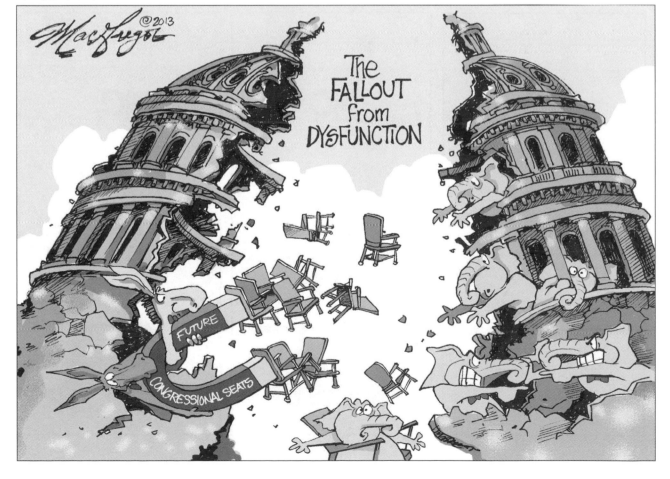

137

TOM TOMORROW
This Modern World

CHUCK LEGGE
The Frontiersman (Alaska)

MIKE LESTER
Washington Post Writers Group

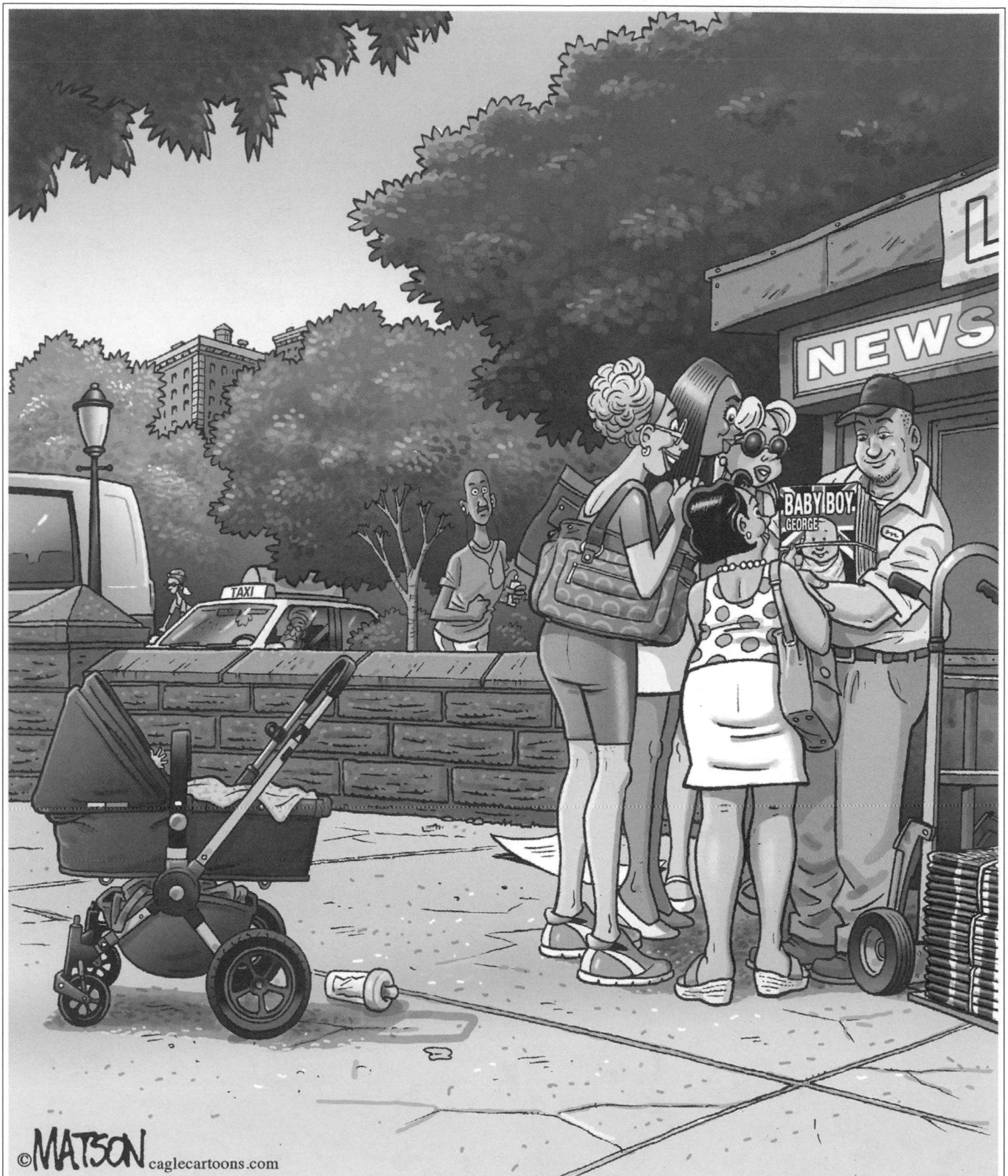

L
NEWS
TAXI
BABY BOY
GEORGE
©MATSON caglecartoons.com

R.J. MATSON
Roll Call

Media / Entertainment

Several news organizations called for more access to President Obama and the White House, claiming that photojournalists were routinely denied the right to photograph or videotape the president while he was performing his official duties. President Obama had promised that his administration would be the most transparent in history.

The mainstream media, generally viewed as supporters of President Obama, seemed to turn against him after the bungled rollout of the Affordable Care Act. Print media, especially newspapers, continued to decline in 2013. Social media is helping fill the gap via computer. Twitter has become an integral part of journalism. Jeff Bezos, founder of Amazon, purchased the *Washington Post,* a venerable and acclaimed newspaper.

"Duck Dynasty" dad Phil Robertson was suspended from filming the television series after making what some regarded as anti-gay comments. The bearded family of the reality series has become a wildly popular fixture in American culture. Singer Miley Cyrus shocked fans with a vulgar dance and costume at the Video Music Awards. One of the hit movies of the year was *Life of Pi,* a computer-animated drama about a boy, a boat, and a tiger.

Celebrity chef Paula Deen lost many of her sponsors and a television show after acknowledging having used racial slang decades ago. Prince George was born to Prince William and Kate Middleton of England.

GLENN FODEN
Media Research Center

CHIP BOK
Creators.com

LISA BENSON
Washington Post Writers Group

STEVE LINDSTROM
Duluth News-Tribune

DAVE SATTLER
Lafayette Journal-Courier (Ind.)

PAUL COMBS
Tribune Media Services

CHRIS BRITT
State-Journal Register (Ill.)

SCOTT STANTIS
Chicago Tribune

ROBERT UNELL
Kansas City Star

DAVID HORSEY
Los Angeles Times

MISTAKES WERE MADE.
AND, FOR THAT, WE'RE SORRY.
BENGHAZI
60
MINUTES
©Taylor Jones - all rights reserved.
caglecartoons.com

TAYLOR JONES
Caglecartoons.com

SHOCKING!
ALARMING!
HORRIBLE!
SYRIA
HANNAH MONTANA:
BREAKING BAD?

NICK ANDERSON
Houston Chronicle

MILT PRIGGEE
Caglecartoons.com

MOBILE -
TABLETS,
SMART PHONES,
ETC...
NEWS-PAPERS
TVs
PCs
PCs SALES DROP BY 14%
CAGLECARTOONS

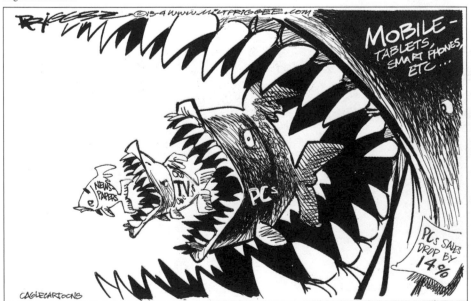

MIKE BECKOM
Index-Journal (Ind.)

J.R. ROSE
Byrd Newspapers of Virginia

147

JIM SIERGEY
jimsiergey.com

ERIC ALLIE
Caglecartoons.com

J.R. ROSE
Byrd Newspapers of Virginia

JEFF HICKMAN
Reno Gazette-Journal

JOSEPH HOFFECKER
Cincinnati Business Courier

GUS RODRIGUEZ
Garrinchatoons.com

DAVID HITCH
Worcester Telegram & Gazette

JOEL PETT
Lexington Herald-Leader

Religion

Cardinal Jorge Mario Bergoglio of Argentina was elected the 266th pope of the Roman Catholic Church on March 13, 2013, assuming the title of Pope Francis in honor of Saint Francis of Assisi. In assuming the office, he became the first Jesuit pope, the first pope from the Americas, and the first pope from the Southern Hemisphere.

He replaced Pope Benedict XVI, who resigned the position, the first pope to do so since 1415 and the first pope to depart voluntarily since 1294. He was said to be the first non-European pontiff in more than 700 years.

Francis is known for his expressions of compassion, kindness, humility, mercy, and commitment to the poor and needy. His major challenges will likely include defending church doctrine on abortion, contraception, and gay marriage.

JIM SIERGEY
jimsiergey.com

THE RACE FOR THE PAPAL CROWN

JIM MORIN
Miami Herald

PAUL BERGE
Q Syndicate

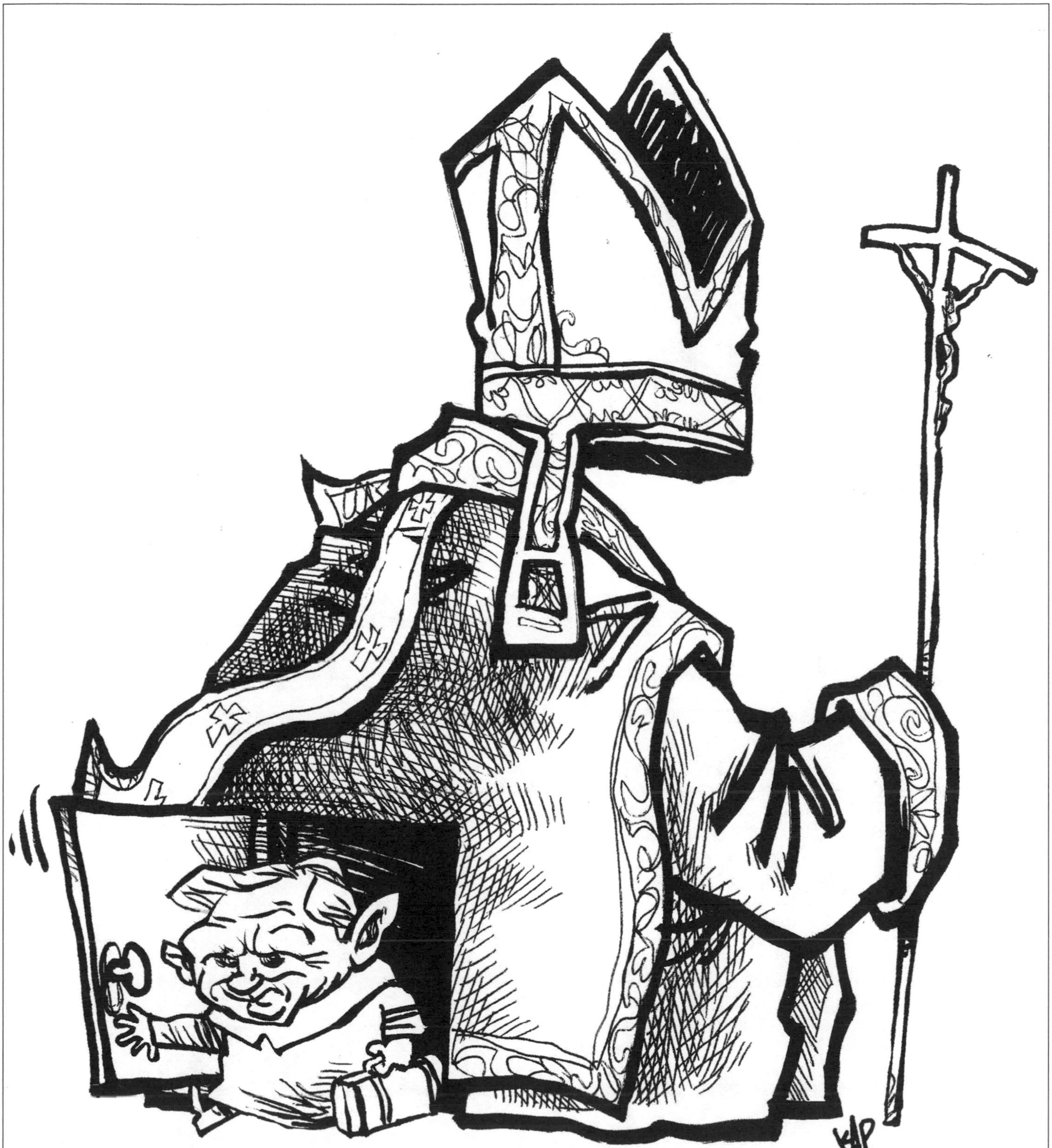
KAP
KAP CAPDEVILA
Caglecartoons.com

DENNIS GALVEZ
Philippine News

ANGELO LOPEZ
Philippines Today

Society

Smart phones and small tablet computers continued to take a larger share of the tech market, putting the squeeze on sales of laptops and desktop computers. Sites such as Facebook and Twitter were becoming more popular than "outdated" email. A social phenomenon, the "selfie," a photograph taken of oneself, blossomed with the proliferation of smart phones.

Thousands of people turned out in the streets of San Francisco to cheer for Batkid, a five-year-old boy with leukemia, and help make his wish to be Batman for a day come true. The Make-a-Wish Foundation created an entire day to fulfill the young boy's dream.

The bullying problem in schools continued to grow in 2013, and even reached the National Football League. America celebrated the 40th anniversary of *Roe v. Wade,* Twinkies returned to supermarket shelves, and Saturday mail delivery seemed destined to be a thing of the past. A key part of the Voting Rights Act of 1965 was struck down, and, in Philadelphia, a doctor was handed a life sentence after a botched abortion. Some cities began discussions on whether teachers should be armed.

In Bangladesh, a huge clothing factory collapsed, killing some 1,000 people.

PETAR PISMETROVIC
Caglecartoons.com

JIM MORIN
Miami Herald

SCOTT STANTIS
Chicago Tribune

JIM DYKE
News-Tribune (Mo.)

MIKE BECKOM
Index-Journal (Ind.)

IRENE OLDS
Courtesy Irene Olds

PETER EVANS
The Islander News (Fla.)

STEVE NEASE
neasecartoons

JOE MOHR
Joe Mohr.com

ED HALL
Artizans.com

JOSEPH HOFFECKER
Cincinnati Business Courier

159

JEFF STAHLER
GOCOMICS.COM

JIMMY MARGULIES
The Record (N.J.)

CHARLES BEYL
Lancaster Sunday News (Pa.)

STEVE NEASE
neasecartoons

GARY VARVEL
Indianapolis Star

ADAM ZYGLIS
Buffalo News

JEFF PARKER
Parkertoons

KATE SALLEY PALMER
Artizans.com

MICHAEL RAMIREZ
Investor's Business Daily

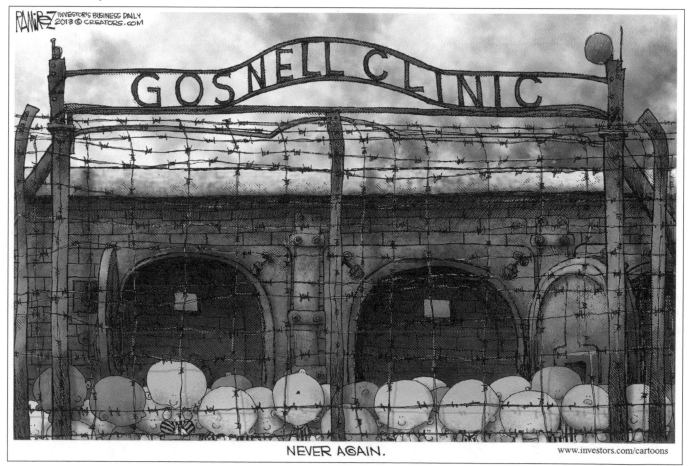

GENE HERNDON
Kokomo Tribune

JON RICHARDS
polcartoons@yahoo.com

CHAN LOWE
South Florida Sun-Sentinel

"CAN I HAVE MY ALLOWANCE IN TWITTER STOCK?"

DANIEL FENECH
Saline Reporter (Mich.)

DAVID COHEN
Asheville Citizen-Times (N.C.)

GENE HERNDON
Kokomo Tribune

MATT BORS
Medium

DON LANDGREN, JR.
Telegram & Gazette (Mass.)

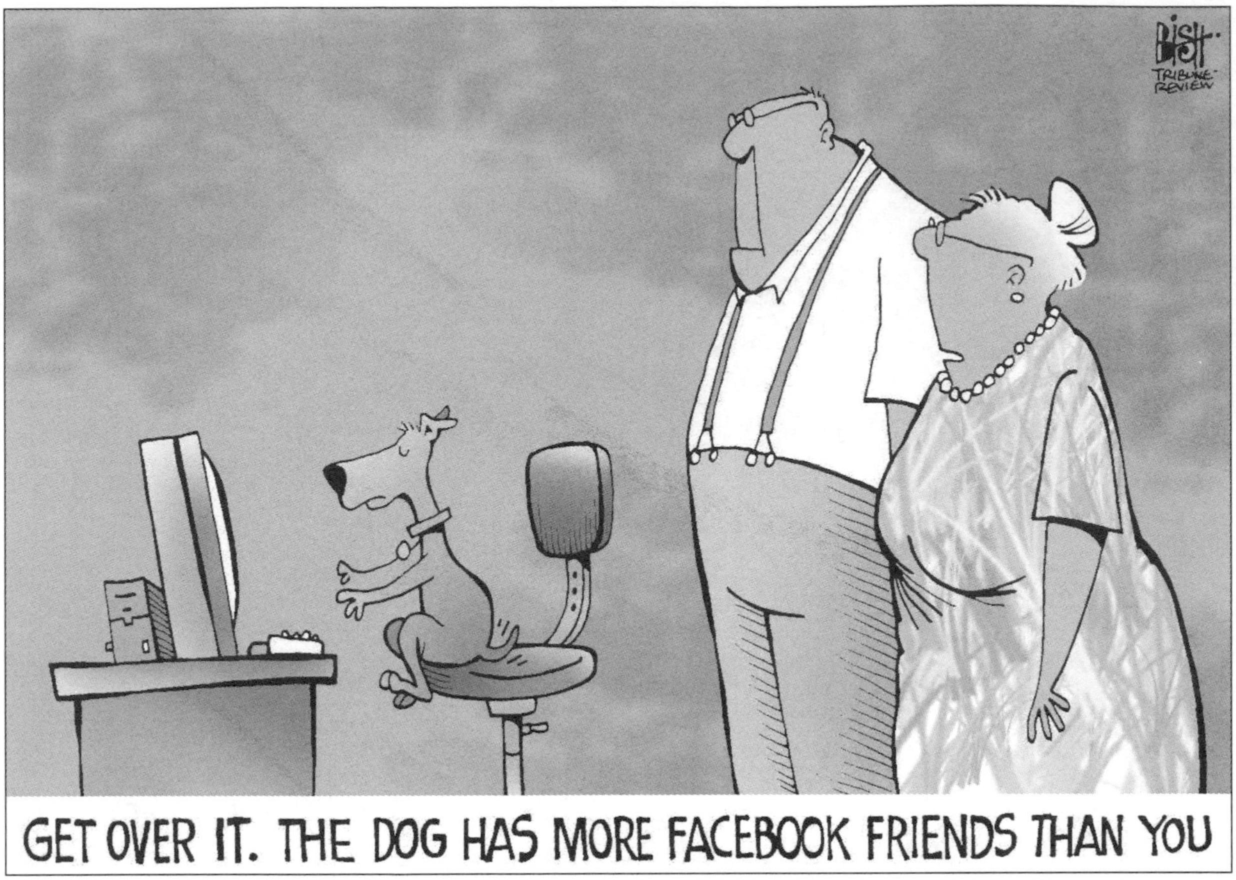
BISH
TRIBUNE-REVIEW
GET OVER IT. THE DOG HAS MORE FACEBOOK FRIENDS THAN YOU

RANDY BISH
Tribune-Review (Pa.)

JIM DYKE
News-Tribune (Mo.)

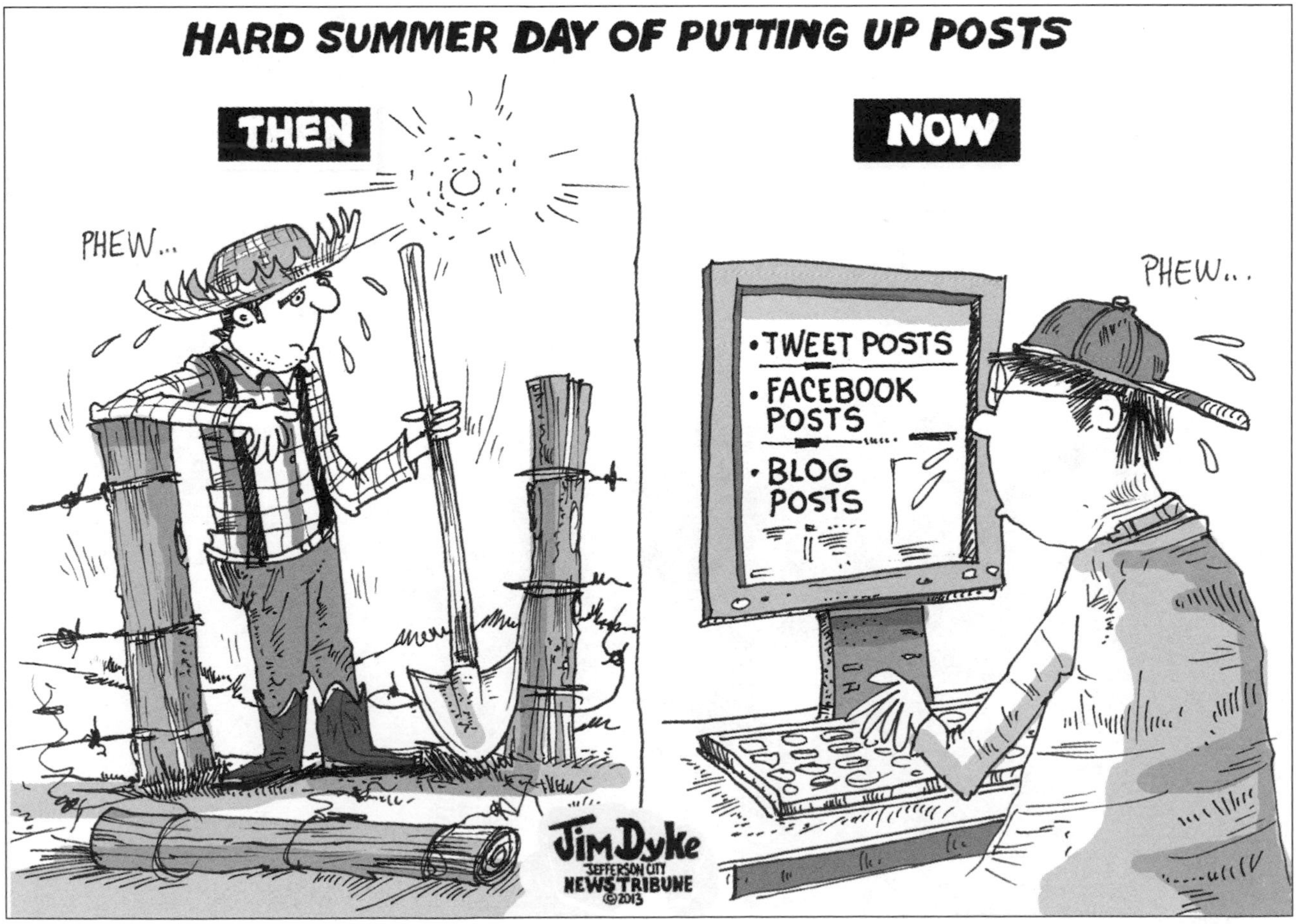
HARD SUMMER DAY OF PUTTING UP POSTS
THEN
NOW
PHEW...
PHEW...
•TWEET POSTS
•FACEBOOK POSTS
•BLOG POSTS
Jim Dyke
JEFFERSON CITY
NEWS TRIBUNE
©2013

JEFF PARKER
Parkertoons

TIM EAGAN
timeagan.com

GEORGE DANBY
Bangor Daily News (Me.)

ED HALL
Artizans.com

NEIL GRAHAME
Spencer Newspapers

DON LANDGREN, JR.
Telegram & Gazette (Mass.)

RANDY BISH
Tribune-Review (Pa.)

CHARLES BEYL
Lancaster Sunday News (Pa.)

MATT BORS
Medium

Sports

Miami Dolphins offensive tackle Jonathan Martin accused teammate Richie Incognito of bullying and hazing. Incognito was suspended by the team after a voicemail to Martin was released containing a racial slur. Martin left the team and underwent counseling for emotional issues. Incognito denied bullying Martin and filed a grievance against the Dolphins. The incident became a media event, and played into concerns about bullying and hazing in the nation's culture.

Controversy continued to surround the Washington Redskins' nickname. Some American Indian groups are said to find the name offensive. Others say they like it. The owner says he plans to keep it.

Wrestling was eliminated as an Olympic sport, but was later restored for 2020 competition. The 2020 Games will be held in Tokyo.

Steroids and other performance-enhancing drugs continued to plague several professional sports, particularly major league baseball. But for professional football, injuries—particularly head injuries—were the major focus. It appeared that more rules changes by the National Football League were coming in an effort to reduce the number and severity of blows to the head.

MILT PRIGGEE
Caglecartoons.com

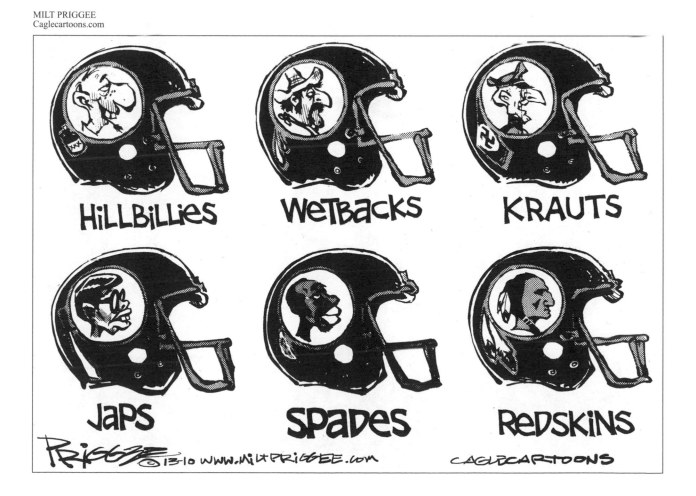

CHRIS BRITT
State-Journal Register (Ill.)

JEFF PARKER
Parkertoons

GUS RODRIGUEZ
Garrinchatoons.com

WILLIAM O'TOOLE
Courtesy William O'Toole

STEVE BREEN
San Diego Union-Tribune

DANIEL FENECH
Saline Reporter (Mich.)

THE POLITICALLY CORRECT NICKNAME FOR THE PRO FOOTBALL TEAM FROM OUR NATION'S CAPITOL!

the washington Pigskins

PORK

THE HAWGS

Congress

TIM BENSON 2013

TIM BENSON
Sioux Falls Argus-Leader (S.D.)

AL GOODWYN
Courtesy Al Goodwyn

177

TIM CAMPBELL
Current Publishing

BRUCE MACKINNON
Halifax Herald (Can.)

PAUL COMBS
Tribune Content Agency

MATT WUERKER
Politico

DAVID DONAR
politicalgraffiti.wordpress.com

WILLIAM O'TOOLE
Courtesy William O'Toole

TOM STIGLICH
Creators Syndicate

Archaic Symbols of Pride and Heritage

Spying

Edward Snowden, a former contractor for the National Security Agency, disclosed operations of a U.S. government mass surveillance program called PRISM. Snowden fled the country to avoid prosecution, and was granted temporary asylum in Russia. The PRISM spy program included the storage of information collected from internet history, telephone calls, and texts of more than a billion people worldwide.

With the help of a London newspaper, Snowden published a collection of articles indicating that major telecom companies had been providing the government with metadata for calls between private U.S. citizens.

Domestically, the NSA monitors phone calls of more than 120 million Verizon subscribers, under a secret interpretation of the Patriot Act. Members of Congress were unaware of these programs, and were denied access to information about them. Director of National Intelligence James Clapper testified before Congress that the NSA doesn't wittingly collect data on Americans, but later admitted that statement was false. In December a federal judge ruled that NSA spying was an unconstitutional invasion of privacy.

The NSA claimed that its intercepts have been instrumental in preventing more than fifty-four terrorist "events," including thirteen in the U.S.

BOB GORRELL
Creators Syndicate

STEVE MCBRIDE
Independence Daily Reporter (Kan.)

JERRY BARNETT
Boonville Standard (Ind.)

KAP CAPDEVILA
Caglecartoons.com

DAVID FITZSIMMONS
The Arizona Star

TOM STIGLICH
Creators Syndicate

TIM HARTMAN
timhartman.com

STEVE SACK
The Star Tribune (Minn.)

TED RALL
Universal Uclick

JEFF DARCY
The Plain Dealer (Oh.)

NICK ANDERSON
Houston Chronicle

NATE BEELER
Columbus Dispatch

M. WUERKER

POLITICO Universal Uclick

MATT WUERKER
Politico

ED HALL
Artizans.com

187

J.R. ROSE
Byrd Newspapers of Virginia

LYNN CARLSON and BILL SMITH
Lompoc Record

MIKE SMITH
Las Vegas Sun

JOE LICCAR
Examiner-Gatehouse Media

BRUCE PLANTE
Tulsa World Media Co.

BILL DAY
Caglecartoons.com

ROB ROGERS
Pittsburgh Post-Gazette

GARY MCCOY
Caglecartoons.com

KEVIN KALLAUGHER
The Economist

191

SCOTT STANTIS
Chicago Tribune

STEVE BREEN
San Diego Union-Tribune

...and Other Issues

Rape in the military continued to be an issue in 2013. The U.S. Postal Service again lost billions of dollars, the George W. Bush Presidential Library opened in College Station, Texas, and tornadoes rocked storm-weary Oklahoma. Nuclear facility leaks in Fukushima, Japan, held the potential for further disaster, and hydraulic fracking, the fracturing of shale with pressurized liquid in order to release natural gas, remained the center of an ongoing argument.

Former Vice-President Dick Cheney remained a favorite target for many.

Among notables who passed away in 2013 were astronaut Neil Armstrong, the first man to walk on the moon; former British Prime Minister Margaret Thatcher; film critic Roger Ebert; actress Annette Funicello; and South African anti-apartheid icon Nelson Mandela.

NICK ANDERSON
Houston Chronicle

MIKE PETERS
Dayton Daily News

JIM MORIN
Miami Herald

DAVE SATTLER
Lafayette Journal-Courier (Ind.)

ROBERT ARIAIL
Universal Uclick

JOEL PETT
Lexington Herald-Leader

WILLIAM FLINT
Dallas Morning News

TIM HARTMAN
timhartman.com

196

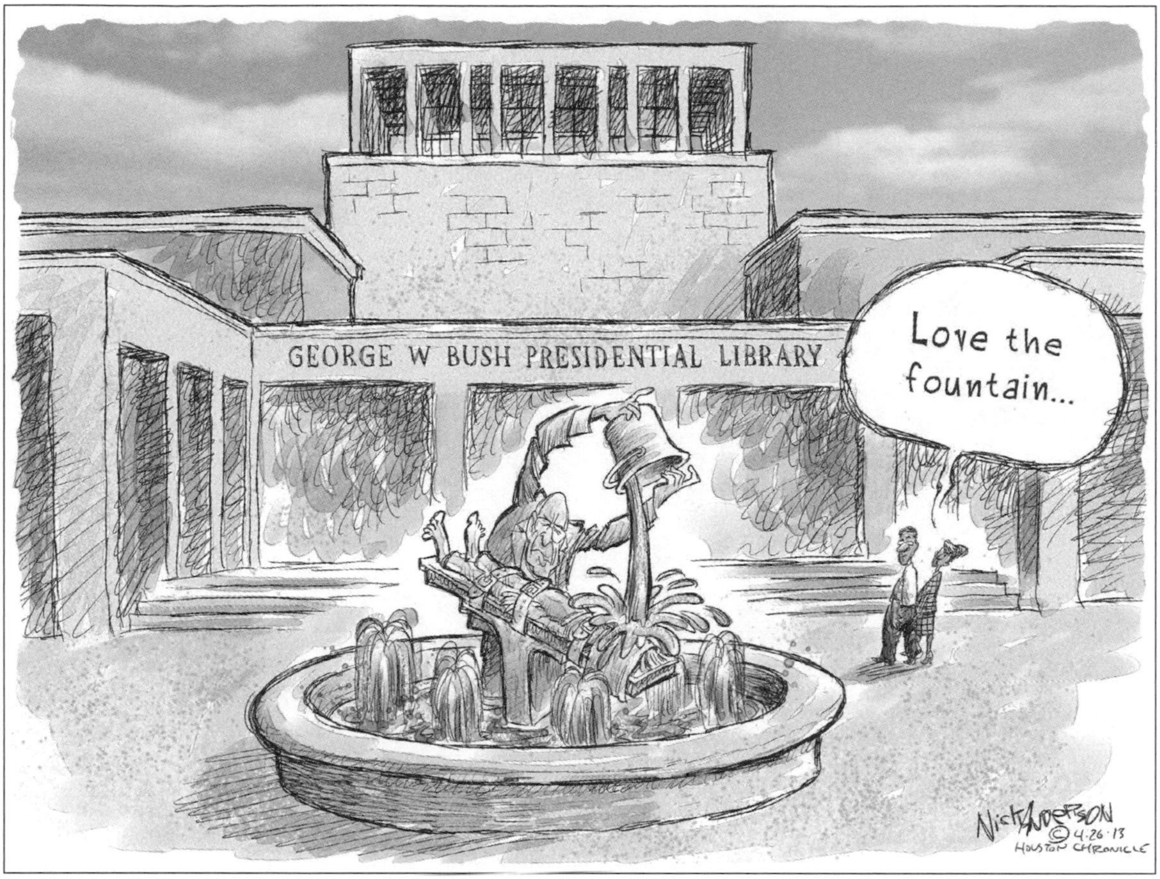
GEORGE W BUSH PRESIDENTIAL LIBRARY
Love the fountain...
NickAnderson ©4-26-13 Houston Chronicle

NICK ANDERSON
Houston Chronicle

MILT PRIGGEE
Caglecartoons.com

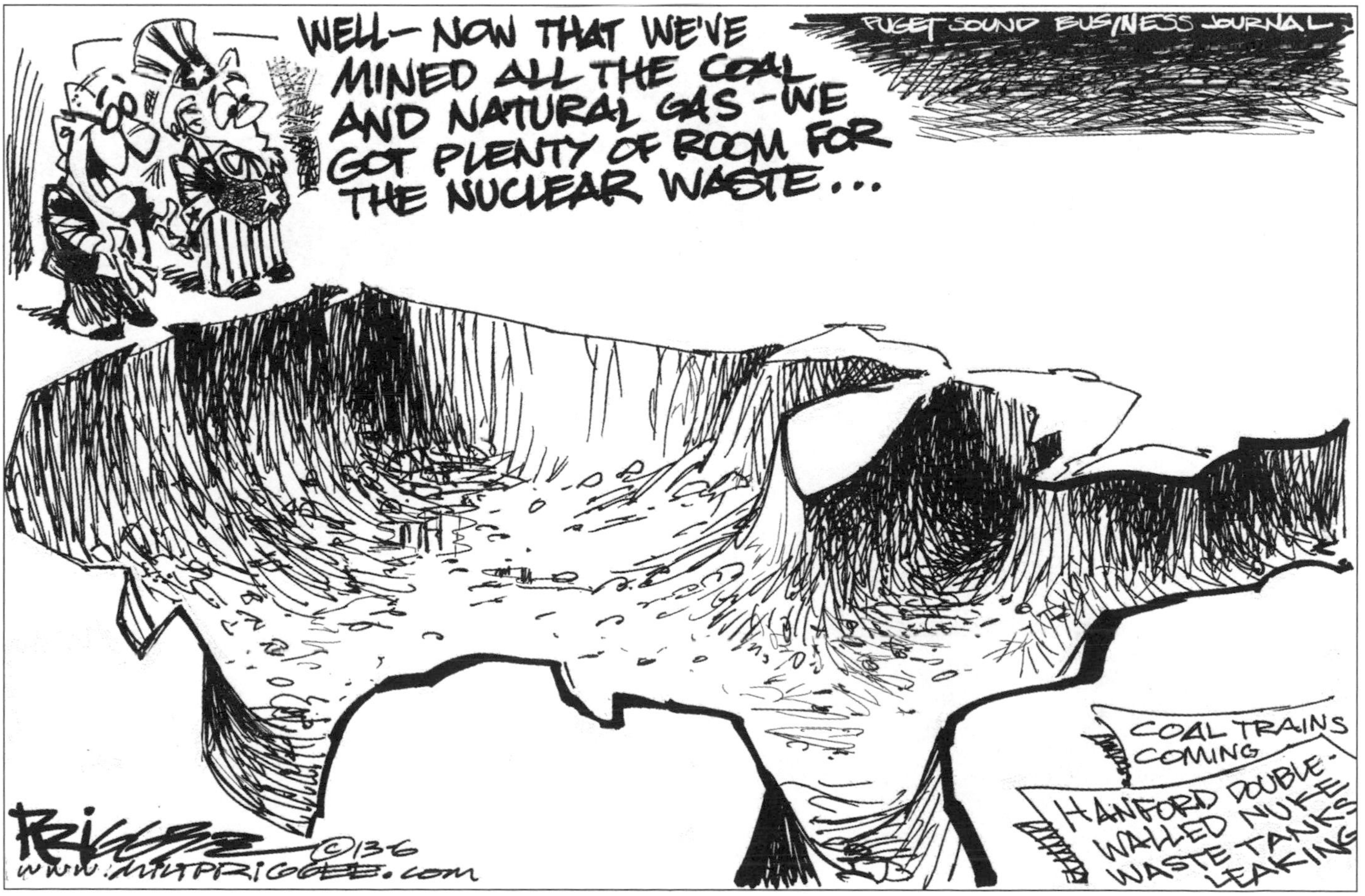
WELL— NOW THAT WE'VE MINED ALL THE COAL AND NATURAL GAS — WE GOT PLENTY OF ROOM FOR THE NUCLEAR WASTE...
PUGET SOUND BUSINESS JOURNAL
COAL TRAINS COMING
HANFORD DOUBLE-WALLED NUKE WASTE TANKS LEAKING
PRIGGEE ©13
www.miltpriggee.com

MIKE SMITH
Las Vegas Sun

PAUL COMBS
Tribune Media Services

LUOJIE
Caglecartoons.com

LUOJIE
Caglecartoons.com

DOES ANYONE ELSE WANT TO KNOW WHAT DAY IT IS?

RANDY BISH
Tribune-Review (Pa.)

JOEL PETT
Lexington Herald-Leader

BUT ON THE BRIGHT SIDE, THE ECONOMY IS MARGINALIZING ALL RACES, OPRAH AND LEBRON ARE MEGA-RICH AND WE ELECTED A HALF-BLACK PRESIDENT!

WAGES
BLACK JOBLESS
PRISON POP.
NON NON-VIOLENCE
ETC.
FAMILY BREAKUPS

8/23/13 LEXINGTON HERALD-LEADER

TOM BECK
Shaw Media

SCOTT COFFMAN
Courier-Journal (Ky.)

ED GAMBLE
King Features Syndicate

JEFF HICKMAN
Reno Gazette-Journal

TOM BECK
Shaw Media

STEVE BREEN
San Diego Union-Tribune

Past Award Winners

PULITZER PRIZE

1922—Rollin Kirby, New York World
1923—No award given
1924—J.N. Darling, New York Herald-Tribune
1925—Rollin Kirby, New York World
1926—D.R. Fitzpatrick, St. Louis Post-Dispatch
1927—Nelson Harding, Brooklyn Eagle
1928—Nelson Harding, Brooklyn Eagle
1929—Rollin Kirby, New York World
1930—Charles Macauley, Brooklyn Eagle
1931—Edmund Duffy, Baltimore Sun
1932—John T. McCutcheon, Chicago Tribune
1933—H.M. Talburt, Washington Daily News
1934—Edmund Duffy, Baltimore Sun
1935—Ross A. Lewis, Milwaukee Journal
1936—No award given
1937—C.D. Batchelor, New York Daily News
1938—Vaughn Shoemaker, Chicago Daily News
1939—Charles G. Werner, Daily Oklahoman
1940—Edmund Duffy, Baltimore Sun
1941—Jacob Burck, Chicago Times
1942—Herbert L. Block, NEA
1943—Jay N. Darling, New York Herald-Tribune
1944—Clifford K. Berryman, Washington Star
1945—Bill Mauldin, United Features Syndicate
1946—Bruce Russell, Los Angeles Times
1947—Vaughn Shoemaker, Chicago Daily News
1948—Reuben L. ("Rube") Goldberg, New York Sun
1949—Lute Pease, Newark Evening News
1950—James T. Berryman, Washington Star
1951—Reginald W. Manning, Arizona Republic
1952—Fred L. Packer, New York Mirror
1953—Edward D. Kuekes, Cleveland Plain Dealer
1954—Herbert L. Block, Washington Post
1955—Daniel R. Fitzpatrick, St. Louis Post-Dispatch
1956—Robert York, Louisville Times
1957—Tom Little, Nashville Tennessean
1958—Bruce M. Shanks, Buffalo Evening News
1959—Bill Mauldin, St. Louis Post-Dispatch
1960—No award given
1961—Carey Orr, Chicago Tribune
1962—Edmund S. Valtman, Hartford Times
1963—Frank Miller, Des Moines Register
1964—Paul Conrad, Denver Post
1965—No award given
1966—Don Wright, Miami News
1967—Patrick B. Oliphant, Denver Post
1968—Eugene Gray Payne, Charlotte Observer
1969—John Fischetti, Chicago Daily News

1970—Thomas F. Darcy, Newsday
1971—Paul Conrad, Los Angeles Times
1972—Jeffrey K. MacNelly, Richmond News Leader
1973—No award given
1974—Paul Szep, Boston Globe
1975—Garry Trudeau, Universal Press Syndicate
1976—Tony Auth, Philadelphia Enquirer
1977—Paul Szep, Boston Globe
1978—Jeff MacNelly, Richmond News Leader
1979—Herbert Block, Washington Post
1980—Don Wright, Miami News
1981—Mike Peters, Dayton Daily News
1982—Ben Sargent, Austin American-Statesman
1983—Dick Locher, Chicago Tribune
1984—Paul Conrad, Los Angeles Times
1985—Jeff MacNelly, Chicago Tribune
1986—Jules Feiffer, Universal Press Syndicate
1987—Berke Breathed, Washington Post Writers Group
1988—Doug Marlette, Atlanta Constitution
1989—Jack Higgins, Chicago Sun-Times
1990—Tom Toles, Buffalo News
1991—Jim Borgman, Cincinnati Enquirer
1992—Signe Wilkinson, Philadelphia Daily News
1993—Steve Benson, Arizona Republic
1994—Michael Ramirez, Memphis Commercial Appeal
1995—Mike Luckovich, Atlanta Constitution
1996—Jim Morin, Miami Herald
1997—Walt Handelsman, New Orleans Times-Picayune
1998—Steve Breen, Asbury Park Press
1999—David Horsey, Seattle Post-Intelligencer
2000—Joel Pett, Lexington Herald-Leader
2001—Ann Telnaes, Tribune Media Services
2002—Clay Bennett, Christian Science Monitor
2003—David Horsey, Seattle Post-Intelligencer
2004—Matt Davies, The Journal News
2005—Nick Anderson, Louisville Courier-Journal
2006—Mike Luckovich, Atlanta Journal-Constitution
2007—Walt Handelsman, Newsday
2008—Michael Ramirez, Investors Business Daily
2009—Steve Breen, San Diego Tribune
2010—Mark Fiore, SFGate.com
2011—Mike Keefe, Denver Post
2012—Matt Wuerker, Politico
2013—Steve Sack, Minneapolis Star Tribune

SIGMA DELTA CHI AWARD

1942—Jacob Burck, Chicago Times
1943—Charles Werner, Chicago Sun
1944—Henry Barrow, Associated Press
1945—Reuben L. Goldberg, New York Sun
1946—Dorman H. Smith, NEA
1947—Bruce Russell, Los Angeles Times
1948—Herbert Block, Washington Post
1949—Herbert Block, Washington Post
1950—Bruce Russell, Los Angeles Times
1951—Herbert Block, Washington Post and
    Bruce Russell, Los Angeles Times
1952—Cecil Jensen, Chicago Daily News
1953—John Fischetti, NEA
1954—Calvin Alley, Memphis Commercial Appeal
1955—John Fischetti, NEA
1956—Herbert Block, Washington Post
1957—Scott Long, Minneapolis Tribune
1958—Clifford H. Baldowski, Atlanta Constitution
1959—Charles G. Brooks, Birmingham News
1960—Dan Dowling, New York Herald-Tribune
1961—Frank Interlandi, Des Moines Register
1962—Paul Conrad, Denver Post
1963—William Mauldin, Chicago Sun-Times
1964—Charles Bissell, Nashville Tennessean
1965—Roy Justus, Minneapolis Star
1966—Patrick Oliphant, Denver Post
1967—Eugene Payne, Charlotte Observer
1968—Paul Conrad, Los Angeles Times
1969—William Mauldin, Chicago Sun-Times
1970—Paul Conrad, Los Angeles Times
1971—Hugh Haynie, Louisville Courier-Journal
1972—William Mauldin, Chicago Sun-Times
1973—Paul Szep, Boston Globe
1974—Mike Peters, Dayton Daily News
1975—Tony Auth, Philadelphia Enquirer
1976—Paul Szep, Boston Globe
1977—Don Wright, Miami News
1978—Jim Borgman, Cincinnati Enquirer

1979—John P. Trever, Albuquerque Journal
1980—Paul Conrad, Los Angeles Times
1981—Paul Conrad, Los Angeles Times
1982—Dick Locher, Chicago Tribune
1983—Rob Lawlor, Philadelphia Daily News
1984—Mike Lane, Baltimore Evening Sun
1985—Doug Marlette, Charlotte Observer
1986—Mike Keefe, Denver Post
1987—Paul Conrad, Los Angeles Times
1988—Jack Higgins, Chicago Sun-Times
1989—Don Wright, Palm Beach Post
1990—Jeff MacNelly, Chicago Tribune
1991—Walt Handelsman, New Orleans Times-
    Picayune
1992—Robert Ariail, Columbia State
1993—Herbert Block, Washington Post
1994—Jim Borgman, Cincinnati Enquirer
1995—Michael Ramirez, Memphis Commercial
    Appeal
1996—Paul Conrad, Los Angeles Times
1997—Michael Ramirez, Los Angeles Times
1998—Jack Higgins, Chicago Sun-Times
1999—Mike Thompson, Detroit Free Press
2000—Nick Anderson, Louisville Courier-Journal
2001—Clay Bennett, Christian Science Monitor
2002—Mike Thompson, Detroit Free Press
2003—Steve Sack, Minneapolis Star-Tribune
2004—John Sherffius, jsherffius@aol.com
2005—Mike Luckovich, Atlanta Journal-Constitution
2006—Mike Lester, Rome News-Tribune
2007—Michael Ramirez, Investors Business Daily
2008—Chris Britt, State Journal-Register
2009—Jack Ohman, The Oregonian
2010—Stephanie McMillan, Code Green
2011—Matt Bors, Universal Uclick
2012—Scott Stantis, Chicago Tribune and
    Phil Hands, Wisconsin State Journal

Index of Cartoonists

Complete Your
CARTOON COLLECTION

Previous editions of this timeless
classic are available for those
wishing to update their
collection of the most
provocative moments
of the past four decades.
Most important, in the end, the wit and
wisdom of the editorial cartoonists prevail on the
pages of these opinion editorials, where one can find memories
and much, much more in the work of the nation's finest cartoonists.

Select from the following supply of past editions

_____1972 Edition	$20.00 pb (F)	_____1988 Edition	$20.00 pb	_____2003 Edition	$14.95 pb
_____1974 Edition	$20.00 pb (F)	_____1989 Edition	$20.00 pb (F)	_____2004 Edition	$14.95 pb
_____1975 Edition	$20.00 pb (F)	_____1990 Edition	$20.00 pb	_____2005 Edition	$14.95 pb
_____1976 Edition	$20.00 pb (F)	_____1991 Edition	$20.00 pb	_____2006 Edition	$14.95 pb
_____1977 Edition	$20.00 pb (F)	_____1992 Edition	$20.00 pb	_____2007 Edition	$14.95 pb
_____1978 Edition	$20.00 pb (F)	_____1993 Edition	$20.00 pb	_____2008 Edition	$14.95 pb
_____1979 Edition	$20.00 pb (F)	_____1994 Edition	$20.00 pb	_____2009 Edition	$14.95 pb
_____1980 Edition	$20.00 pb (F)	_____1995 Edition	$20.00 pb	_____2010 Edition	$14.95 pb
_____1981 Edition	$20.00 pb (F)	_____1996 Edition	$20.00 pb	_____2011 Edition	$14.95 pb
_____1982 Edition	$20.00 pb (F)	_____1997 Edition	$20.00 pb	_____2012 Edition	$14.95 pb
_____1983 Edition	$20.00 pb (F)	_____1998 Edition	$20.00 pb	_____2013 Edition	$14.95 pb
_____1984 Edition	$20.00 pb (F)	_____1999 Edition	$20.00 pb	_____Add me to the list of standing	
_____1985 Edition	$20.00 pb (F)	_____2000 Edition	$20.00 pb	orders	
_____1986 Edition	$20.00 pb (F)	_____2001 Edition	$20.00 pb		
_____1987 Edition	$20.00 pb	_____2002 Edition	$14.95 pb		

**TO PLACE AN ORDER
CALL 1-800-843-1724,**
visit our Web site at www.pelicanpub.com, or
e-mail us at sales@pelicanpub.com